OUT OF NAZARETH

OUT OF NAZARETH

A SELECTION OF SERMONS AND LECTURES

BY

DONALD M. BAILLIE

Late Professor of Systematic Theology
in the University of St. Andrews

THE SAINT ANDREW PRESS

EDINBURGH

Published in 1958 by
The Saint Andrew Press
121 George Street, Edinburgh 2
Printed by
Robert Cunningham and Sons Ltd., Alva
and bound by
Hunter and Foulis Ltd., Edinburgh 7

NOTE

Here is a further selection of sermons and occasional addresses made, like the former, from the considerable mass of manuscript material, none of it intended for publication, which was found in Donald Baillie's study after his death in 1954.

There has been added that part of his ordinary lectures to theological students which deals with the doctrine of the Trinity. A sermon on this doctrine was printed in the earlier selection *To Whom Shall We Go?* The doctrine was also dealt with briefly in one of the pieces printed in the other posthumous volume *The Theology of the Sacraments* (Faber and Faber, 1957); and one of the sermons in the present volume deals with 'The Mystery of the Trinity'. A desire has, however, been expressed that the author's fuller teaching on this subject should be made available. The lectures were written, as was his habit, in pen and ink in a manuscript book, and were really in the form of a teacher's notes, meant for no eye but his own. A certain amount of editing has therefore been necessary. Underlinings have been largely ignored; some colloquialisms have been made to disappear; a few footnote references have been supplied; some repetitions, such as were doubtless necessary for classroom teaching, have been removed; two short sections have been omitted, as dealing with matters of more specialized theological interest; and a few other passages have been recast in a somewhat more compressed form. Care has, however, been taken that in no case should there be any alteration of meaning.

Some of the sermons here included have already appeared in *The British Weekly* and *The Expository Times* and thanks are due to the editors of these journals for their willingness to have them reprinted.

CONTENTS

SERMONS

vii

LECTURES

SERMONS

1. OUT OF NAZARETH

And Nathanael said unto him, Can there be any good thing come out of Nazareth? Philip saith unto him, Come and see.   JOHN 1.46

'CAN any good thing come out of Nazareth?' We don't know whether there was anything against Nazareth, any special reason why it should have been treated in such a slighting way, as a place where you wouldn't expect anything very beautiful to blossom.

There was nothing wrong with the situation of Nazareth: you can see it there yet, nestling in a little pocket on the side of a hill which commands an extensive and beautiful view. It wouldn't be bad for a child to grow up in such a spot.

But certainly Nazareth had never been remarkable for anything in the way of religion. It had never produced a great man, a prophet, a man of God. It is never even mentioned in the Old Testament at all, which means that it hadn't any notable religious and historical associations. There weren't any heroic stories that could have been told about its past. Moreover, it was a little country town, and you know the saying that 'if God made the country and man made the town, the Devil made the little country town'. Nazareth may not have been any worse than the rest. It is Nathanael in this chapter who asks: 'Can any good thing come out of Nazareth?'

Well, you see, Nathanael himself belonged to the neighbouring village of Cana; and you know how it often is in a country district, how neighbouring villages are rather apt to look down on each other, so that even the guileless Nathanael was a little suspicious when Nazareth was mentioned—didn't think it likely that anything very notable and beautiful would

I

hail from that quarter. He couldn't imagine the drab old village of Nazareth blossoming in such a way.

As a matter of fact, it was much the same with the people of Nazareth themselves: we discover that from another passage in the Gospels. Even they didn't expect Nazareth to produce anything very wonderful. No doubt they were fond enough of their village, and they wouldn't stand any nonsense about it from the people of Cana or any neighbouring village. But after all, life was pretty hard and secular in Nazareth. They felt it wasn't a place that would ever run very much to religion or heroism. They didn't expect that of themselves and they didn't even encourage it.

When one day Jesus, in the course of His ministry, went back to Nazareth, where He had been brought up, He didn't get much of a reception. They said: 'He's just one of ourselves, he's a Nazarene, he was brought up in the village, and used to be a carpenter, and we've all employed him, and we know his people, his brothers and sisters—they're still in the village; and so *he* can't be much.'

They didn't expect their village to break any records in the way of religious goodness and greatness. They had known too much about commonplace days and commonplace ways in their mean village. Nazareth wasn't the kind of place in which it was easy to be good, or in which Heaven seemed near, or in which wonderful things would be likely to happen. That kind of thing wouldn't hail from Nazareth. How much of human nature there is in all that! Nazareth is not the only place of which it has been said. But Nazareth is the classical instance, because Nazareth is the place that has forever given the lie to all those dreary cynical negations and sceptical questions.

For out of Nazareth, out of dreary commonplace unlikely Nazareth, there did come, by God's grace, the greatest good that has ever come to mankind. In a humble home in

Nazareth, unknown to the world, there grew up Jesus Christ. There He first learnt to walk and to talk, there He played with other boys, there He went to school, there He learnt His trade, from there He went forth at the age of thirty to kindle in the world a flame that is still burning and will never die.

It was a Nazarene that did that. His followers came to be called the Nazarenes. The name of Nazareth became dear with sacred meanings and is now enshrined in the heart of all mankind.

> O sing a song of Nazareth,
>   Of sunny days of joy;
> O sing of fragrant flowers' breath,
>   And of the sinless Boy.
> For now the flowers of Nazareth
>   In every heart may grow;
> Now spreads the fame of His dear Name
>   On all the winds that blow.

That is what has happened, by the grace of God, to the village of which once it was asked: 'Can any good thing come out of Nazareth?'

Now I want to tell you something in my own experience. Years ago in the course of a walking-tour, I was at a little English village called Mamble, on the uplands above the River Teme, on the borders of Shropshire and Worcestershire. I had never heard of it except in one place—John Drinkwater has a poem about it, and that made me curious to go and see it. Drinkwater had never been there himself, but the lazy sound of the name Mamble had tickled his fancy, and this is how his poem goes:

> I never went to Mamble
>   That lies above the Teme,
> So I wonder who's in Mamble,
>   And whether people seem
> Who breed and brew along there
>   As lazy as the name.

3

> And whether any song there
> Sets alehouse wits aflame.
> The finger-post says Mamble
> And that is all I know . . .

And so on. I needn't finish it. But curiosity made me tramp along the road to Mamble, which Drinkwater imagined to be such a lazy sort of place. When I got there, there certainly wasn't much of it: a tiny little village, a few houses, one little shop, an old church, and a little inn.

The inn wasn't very hospitable—they couldn't give me a bed for the night. And it was rather noisy for a Sunday afternoon. I wasn't very sorry to clear out and go to a farm-house outside the village. Mamble wasn't the sort of place one would choose to live in; it was a poor unpromising kind of village.

In the afternoon I walked along to the old village church —partly to find out if there was to be an evening service which I could attend. As I was standing in the doorway, looking around, a lady in black came in at the gate of the churchyard, carrying flowers. I thought she was going to put them in the church. But she walked past the church into the back part of the churchyard, and then I saw that she was putting the flowers on a grave. A few minutes later I spoke to her and asked her about evening service, and that opened a conversation. She was a farmer's wife. They were simple folk, but they had sent their son to Oxford—the only one they had, as their other child had died young. This one was a six-foot youth of brilliant parts and evidently a heart of gold. He was their hope and pride. After three years at St. John's College, Oxford, he had won a travelling scholarship in the interests of international friendship, and had spent a year in France and Germany. Then, just as they were expecting word as to when he would arrive home, they received a telegram to say that he had been accidentally drowned.

4

This was the second anniversary—it had happened just two years ago that Sunday. Some of his friends from a distance were coming to attend evening service in memory of him, and she was putting flowers on his grave. She said he had some wonderful friends at Oxford, and also that he had remained quite simple and unspoilt. She said she believed in the end he would have become some kind of missionary, because his one dream was to use any gifts he had to do a little good in the world. His gifts must have been out-standing. But now that dream was over, and his father and mother had a grave to tend and a golden memory to keep.

That was in Mamble churchyard that Sunday afternoon. It gave one a glimpse of a home and a life, a dream and a memory. Perhaps you think that probably a mother's love somewhat gilded and glorified the picture. That may be. But when I think of Mamble now, it is not just of the lazy name in Drinkwater's poem, and the poor little village and the noisy little inn, but of that little church and churchyard, and that Sunday afternoon, and that story.

What a window it opens! Mamble was an unlikely place for anything notable to happen—lazy Mamble, a mere name on a finger-post, a mean little village. But Mamble had its story to tell of the great simple human things: home, and hopes, and love, and death, and grief and memory; yes, and its story to tell of a keen young life that was given to noble aims and dreams, until it was cut off, or rather (shouldn't we say?) called to higher opportunities in realms unknown. Its training ground for all that was the little village of Mamble. That was where the boy learnt to love the home to which he always remained loyal; that was where he first went to school; that was where he thought the 'long long thoughts' of youth. All that had been going on in Mamble. 'Can any good thing come out of Mamble?' Of course it can; and there it was.

'Nothing very remarkable, after all,' perhaps you think. No, of course it wasn't very remarkable. The thing is the kind of thing that can happen anywhere—is happening everywhere. That is just what I want to tell you. I've told you that simple story, not that we may become sentimental over it (that would be a poor thing to do) but that we may take home its bracing lesson to ourselves, wherever we happen to live.

Almost every one of us knows what it is to settle down into a state of inexpectancy, a habit of not expecting very noble things of ourselves. Our life seems such a common-place thing. The place we live in seems such an unhelpful place. The circumstances in which we are placed seem so unfavourable. We sometimes have a vision of what a truly noble Christian life would be—what it would be to live in this world as one of God's heroes, clean and brave and kind, a son or daughter of God, a knight-errant of His Kingdom. But all that seems very far away from us. It belongs to the time 'when knights were bold', or at least it belongs to more romantic places than the places where we have to live our lives. It belongs to people whose lot is cast more favourably than ours. As for us, what chance have we?

If we could make a new start somewhere else, we might have a chance, but what chance have we here where we are? (Perhaps we don't say all that to ourselves in words, but we say it half-unconsciously.) You don't expect very much of yourself. You hardly expect ever to be much of a Christian, to be a very good pure courageous unselfish man or woman. You hardly expect to be of much use to God or man. You don't take very seriously, as applied to yourself, the great offers and promises of the Gospel. How can all that happen in your unpromising life? Can any good thing come out of Nazareth?

And the answer is: Yes, it can. Out of Nazareth came

6

Jesus Christ, the Son of God. And it was always His way to go here and there, to the most unlikely places, and seek out all sorts and conditions of men and women to make them kings and priests to God.

It might be Nazareth, or Bethsaida, or Jerusalem. And a little later it might be Ephesus or Corinth or Rome. And in our time it might be London or Mamble, or Glasgow, or St. Andrews, or any other place, where your lot is cast, or mine.

Let me ask two questions as I close.

(1) Is there anyone reading this who is going to do a great work some day for God? Well, of course, you can't answer. You don't know. After all, the main thing is not to do great things, but to do God's will. But this is the kind of thing I mean. God's Church on earth always needs foreign missionaries.

That is a great work. It is not profitable financially, it is not safe, it is not easy, it is not a good investment—it has nothing to recommend it except this: that it is better worth doing in itself than anything else in the world. It is unmistakably the work of God. I wonder if there is any one of you who will hear the call to it.

You parents, wondering what your sons and daughters will do when they leave school: what would you say if they told you they were going to be missionaries? Why shouldn't they? Why shouldn't your family provide such an offering to God? And you young people, why not you? In spite of all obstacles. Is there perhaps among you some David Livingstone, some Mary Slessor?

(2) My second question is even more searching: Is there any of you who does not want a place in God's great purpose? There isn't anyone who need be left out, unless you want to leave yourself out. Jesus Christ is 'able to save to the uttermost those who come to God by Him'. God's grace can work in every kind of Nazareth, every kind of life. Without

7

His grace nothing good can come out of anywhere. But by His grace anything may happen anywhere. And His grace is not far from any one of us, to make our lives great and good, beautiful and useful, wherever our lot is cast, if only we will commit our lives to Him.

2. GOD CARRYING HIS PEOPLE

And even to your old age I am he; and even to hoar hairs will I carry you. ISAIAH 46.4

IN this familiar text you have a picture of God carrying His people. But it becomes ever so much more significant when you notice that in the same chapter you have another picture —of people carrying their God. Look on this picture and on that.

On the one hand, people carrying their God. That is meant to be a picture of the religion of the races round about Israel. An Israelite prophet is looking around him in the world, and as he thinks of all that religion means to him, he can't help smiling at the poor kind of religion these other races lived by—he can't help thinking what a miserable thing it must be to have a god who couldn't do anything for you, like the gods of the nations. It isn't the only place in the Old Testament where we find the Hebrews talking like that.

And no wonder. They couldn't help feeling that contrast. So many people in this world seemed to have a god that couldn't do anything for them, or even for himself—they had to do everything for him. 'They bear him upon the shoulder (says this chapter), they carry him, and set him in his place, and he stands; he can't move from his place. Somebody cries to him, but he can't answer, or save a man from his trouble.'

You can see the picture (drawn, surely, with a conscious touch of humour): a great glittering god, made of silver or gold, very glorious-looking, but very heavy, and really just a bit of furniture; and you seem to see half a dozen men, like furniture-men, staggering under the weight of it as they

9

carry it to its place, and glad to put it down. Once it is put down in its place, there it stays. It can't move until they move it (says the prophet), and it won't help to carry its worshippers—they have to carry it. And that is their religion. That is one kind of religion. The people have to carry their god.

And then, on the other hand, in the words of our text, a picture of the Lord God carrying His people, everlastingly, unwearyingly:

> Hearken unto me, O House of Jacob, and all the remnant of the House of Israel, which have been carried by me from your birth, yea, carried from the womb; and even to your old age I am he; and even to hoar hairs will I carry you; I have made, and I will bear; yea, I will carry, and will deliver you.

These two kinds of religion are always with us, even in Christian circles, after all these centuries of the Gospel. Everybody has heard of that sad little conversation between Thomas Carlyle as an old man and his friend James Anthony Froude. It must be told in Froude's own words: 'I once said to him, not long before his death, that I could only believe in a God which did something. With a cry of pain which I shall never forget, he said "He does nothing".'

Doubtless that does not do justice to the religion of Carlyle; but at least it does credit to the old man's depth and honesty that he said it with a cry of pain. For we need a God who can do things. And there you have the whole wide sad difference between two ways of taking our religion: between the kind of religion that is only a burden, to be carried, and the kind which does things for us, carries our burdens and carries us.

Let us think of the two kinds.

(1) *The kind of religion that does nothing for us, but has to be carried as a burden.*

Why is it that young people growing up out of childhood into manhood or womanhood so often let their religion slip off them? After all their Christian training and even their apparent interest in religion, and perhaps their active participation in the communicant membership of the Church of their fathers—after all that, why is it that, when they are quite free to order their lives for themselves, and especially when they move away from home to a different environment, they so often say goodbye to all that, and hardly seem to miss it?

One wonders at it. Why does it happen so often? That is a big question. But mustn't it at least be because, for one reason or another, their religion was not doing anything for them? They had not so learnt religion as to cast themselves upon God. Their religion wasn't enriching and strengthening and beautifying their lives. It was just a tradition laid upon them, a burden to be carried; and so quite naturally, perhaps half-unconsciously, they let it slip off at the first opportunity, and were easier without it—like those men that we pictured setting down the heavy useless god they were carrying, and that was an end of it.

But, to go deeper: there are others who can't lay it down as easily as that, but who nevertheless find it more of a burden than a help. They do take it seriously, but it gives them much more fear and care than peace and joy.

Let me tell you a very penetrating thing that was once said by an American evangelist about the difference between Methodists and Presbyterians in their religious temper. 'A Methodist knows he's got religion, but he's afraid he may lose it. A Presbyterian knows he can't lose it, but he's afraid he hasn't got it.' That saying is much more than witty. It sums up a large part of the historic controversy between the Calvinists and the Arminians. But what I want especially to point out is that in both cases the word 'afraid' comes in.

The one is afraid he'll lose religion; the other is afraid he hasn't got it. As if it were quite the regular thing that a man's religion should keep him perpetually uneasy, burdened with fear and worry.

And isn't it quite true, even in these modern days, of many of the people who take their religion in earnest, even if they wouldn't put it into these words? Isn't it true even of many young folk, or perhaps especially of young folk, though they don't show it to everybody? They may take their religion in earnest, and do a great deal for it, but it doesn't seem to do much for them. It is a bit of a burden. It weighs them down rather than lifts them up.

One way in which this happens, with certain temperaments, is that our religion gets too much tied up with doubting and questioning. Now certainly some people have to pass through that discipline of doubt, usually in the days of youth; and all honour to those who face it manfully. Tennyson was quite right when he said that there lives more faith in honest doubt than in half the Creeds. But, as he knew very well, you can't live indefinitely on that kind of faith. It is not a resting-place, or even a halting-place. Tennyson went on to describe how his friend, the doubter, advanced to something better.

> He fought his doubts and gathered strength,
>   He would not make his judgment blind.
>   He faced the spectres of the mind
> And laid them. Thus he came at length
>
> To find a stronger faith his own.

That is what matters: after doubt, to find a stronger faith your own. Of course you can't get rid of your religious perplexities all at once. But you can't live on religious perplexities. And what a futile thing it is to try to make a religion of them, to become self-conscious about them, to get into the habit of being lost in a wilderness of doubt, always seeking and hardly expecting ever to be very sure of anything!

In all these ways, I say, it is a weary business to have a religion which is only our own effort and struggle, with the constant strain of trying to get hold of something. Nay, we need something that will get hold of us, and keep us, and hold us up. It is a sad weary thing to have a religion which only exhausts us, which is laid upon us as a burden—or a God that does nothing for us, like those men in the ancient picture.

(2) *But now think of the other kind of religion, that can do something for us, carry our burdens and carry us.*

'Even to your old age I am he,' says God, 'and even to hoar hairs will I carry you; I have made, and I will bear; I will carry, and will deliver you.' What music is in those words, when we are tired of seeking! What peace and strength are in that picture of God carrying His people! It is a foreshadowing of the very Gospel of Jesus. It gives us a God who is always beforehand with His people. He made us before ever we thought of Him. He sought us before ever we sought Him. He will carry us if we will cast ourselves upon Him.

I have sometimes thought that this is one of the rediscoveries of our time, evidencing itself in many different quarters, and promising to bring back something of 'the lost radiance of the Christian religion', just this simple fact that the essence of the Gospel lies in God seeking us before we seek Him.

Let me give you some examples, from widely diverse schools, of this glad rediscovery of the meaning of Christianity.

My first witness is a great scholar of our time who is not a Christian at all, but a Jew, which perhaps makes his testimony all the more striking. He is the great Jewish scholar, Dr Montefiore, who has always been wrestling with the question whether there was in the message of Jesus any new and original element that could not be found in any prophet or rabbi before Him. Repeatedly in his books he singles out this one thing as absolutely new: the conception of God actually going out in quest of sinful men who were not seeking Him but were turned away from Him.

No one had ever spoken of God like that until Jesus did (says the Jewish scholar). The prophet Isaiah had indeed pictured God as a shepherd to His people, gathering the lambs in His arms and carrying them in His bosom. But Jesus went further: He pictured the Divine Shepherd going out into the wilderness to seek a lost sheep that could never otherwise have even begun to find the fold. 'And when he hath found it, he layeth it upon his shoulders rejoicing.'

That was Christ's picture of God. That was new; and it is the very heart of Christianity.

Another witness: some years ago the National Christian Council of Japan drew up a document to be presented to a great international conference at Jerusalem in which they tried to set forth the points in which Christianity goes beyond all other religions (and those men in Japan had good reason to know, for they had those other religions all around them, and even in their own blood). Well, this was one of the distinctive and superlative things they saw in the Christian Gospel: 'Man not seeking God, but God taking the initiative in seeking man.' Isn't that striking? The same rediscovery again.

Another witness from a very different quarter: that great Roman Catholic divine of our age, the Baron von Hügel, born of a Scottish mother. He was never tired of dwelling on the Prevenience of God as the very soul of our religion—the doctrine that God is always beforehand with His creatures. He loved to illustrate it by quoting what St. Bernard in the twelfth century used to say to his monks. St. Bernard told his monks that, however early they might wake and rise for prayer in their chapel on a cold mid-winter morning, or even in the dead of night, they would always find God awake before them, waiting for them—nay, it was He that had awakened them to seek His face. And Baron von Hügel goes on to tell us that when in recent years a London non-conformist minister got hold of that truth and preached it, crowds of his hearers flocked to him afterwards to tell him that they had never in their lives heard such doctrine, and how wonderful and awakening it was.

One more witness: it is the very same rediscovery that has been made by the Karl Barth school of theologians which is injecting such new life and power into religious thinking just now (even if one doesn't always agree with their way of putting it). Here is a sentence from one of their leaders: 'This is the absolutely incomparable message of the Gospel, that God comes to man, and that man does not go to God.' The same thing again, as the heart of Christianity! A God who does things for us, anticipates us, comes in quest of us, and carries us all the way.

And now: do you see how all that comes to a head in what we call the doctrine of the Incarnation, that God was incarnate in Jesus Christ?

That sounds very mysterious: and doubtless it has greatly perplexed some of us. But can you see now what a simple thing it means? I have been talking of man's quest of God, which is the supreme thing in the story of the human race. In that perennial quest Jesus of Nazareth was the greatest seeker and finder of all, the very crown and flower of humanity in its upward struggle.

But is that all? Nay, that is never the whole truth. Man could never (we have seen) have been seeking God if God had not been seeking man. That is the other side of it, and it really comes first, for God is always beforehand with us.

And so when at last humanity reached its highest product in ancient Galilee, when humanity on its upward quest broke all its records and out-topped all its highest levels in the supreme path-finder, the man Christ Jesus, it was not simple humanity on its upward quest (that leaves out the best and deepest truth): it was God on His downward quest. It was God coming in quest of humanity, breaking all His records, coming further into the wilderness than ever before, that He might find us and lay us upon His shoulders rejoicing. 'God was in Christ, reconciling the world to himself.'

That is what God is like. That is what He did and does for us in Jesus Christ and will do to the end. He is a God who does things. How it helps us when we discover that that is the meaning of the Incarnation! Then it is no more a doctrine, but a Gospel.

Therefore I say, my friends, do not be content with anything less than that. Do not let yourself think of God more meanly than that. Do not be satisfied with endless hopeless joyless seeking and struggling, when God Himself is seeking and finding and carrying you.

Let Him do it. Remember the Gospel of Jesus. And do not be content with a religion of strain and struggle, and fear and doubt, and heavy hearts and clouded faces, when you may, through the Gospel of Jesus, have a religion that will carry you and carry your burdens and give you strength and joy and peace.

3. THY FATHER WHICH IS IN SECRET

Thy Father which is in secret. MATTHEW 6.6.

As Jesus went through life in this world He saw round about Him a good many people whose religion was entirely a public matter. It hadn't any inward secret side to it. They had no interest in that. They never allowed themselves to be alone with God.

These people might be benevolent; they did good deeds and gave away money for worthy causes. But they always let it be known that they were doing it; that was part of their idea, and they would have felt it was all wasted without that.

They had devotional habits, too: they found time for prayer, but preferably in some public place where they could be seen and make an impression. To pray alone and in secret would have been a dull and profitless business.

They went in for fasting; that is, they had their days of self-denial and self-discipline. But here again they didn't keep it to themselves: they went about with grave, sad faces to let everybody know how devoted they were. That was half the sweetness of the religious life. (We can understand it, can't we? Our own consciences recognize the picture.)

Now all these people thought they were fearing and serving God. But according to Jesus, they were looking for God in the wrong place. And it was in speaking of these things, and to point people to the right place, that Jesus coined this phrase of our text, 'thy Father which is in secret'.

He did not mean that we shouldn't share our religion with our neighbours. Of course we have to share it. But we can't share the secret unless we have it in the lonely depths of our own hearts. He did not mean that we have to hide our light: He said that we must let it shine. Only, not for our own glory, but for the glory of God. He did not mean that the love of God should make us care less for our neighbours: when we want to serve God, it is just in our fellow creatures that we have to find Him. It is only in serving them that we can hope to find Him. It is only in serving them that we can serve Him. Only there is no need to let all the world know of your acts of service; if that is your motive, you are not doing it for God at all. And you can't do anything for God in the world at large unless you have God yourself. You may have public esteem and private popularity and a sociable kind of religion. But if your religion depends on that, and is exhausted in that—well, then, that is your God. You have your reward. But you haven't got the Father who is in secret. You have a substitute. But it isn't God. And you must have God. You must have a faith in Him and a friendship with Him, deep down in the lonely secret of your heart: 'your Father who dwells in secret'.

In the light of that, let me give you three simple truths about the spiritual life.

(1) *Every man's soul is his own secret.* Nobody can get inside your soul except yourself. Surely there is a deep sense in which that is true. It is not the whole truth, for friends can get very close together. But underneath the closest friendship there is a profound loneliness in human life, a deep solitariness of the human soul. A man's soul is his own secret. Little children do not feel it because they have not yet been driven in upon themselves. But as soon as childhood is past, and boys and girls begin to grow up into men and women, they begin to feel it. That age is the time of great friendship. There is a craving for friendship, and friends mean more to one then than ever before or after. But that is just because the awakening of the soul has brought the

feeling of loneliness. And perhaps it is true that the deeper the friendship goes the more is there a background of loneliness which can never disappear. The human friendship may go very deep, and the deeper the better. It is bad for us to be too self-contained and never to have anybody to whom we can speak of the most intimate things. I wish the Christian Church could provide more than it does of that deepest kind of fellowship, to keep people from utter spiritual loneliness. It did in the earliest generations, and why shouldn't it still?

But with all that—in spite of the blessings of fellowship and 'the tie that binds our hearts in Christian love', and however warm and rich and deep the spiritual friendship may be—there always remains an ultimate solitariness of the human soul: a sense of all sorts of unspeakable things that you can never quite communicate to anybody else, never altogether put into words and pass on.

Browning spoke of the 'fancies that broke through language and escaped'. Tennyson sang:

> I sometimes count it half a sin
>> To put in words the grief I feel;
>> For words, like nature, half reveal
> And half conceal the soul within.

And Matthew Arnold compared our separate souls to little islands in an archipelago.

> Yes, in the sea of life enisled,
>> With echoing straits between us thrown,
> Dotting the shoreless watery wild,
>> We mortal millions live alone.

Millions of us, and yet each one alone, because no one can get inside your soul except yourself.

But it isn't only poets that discover it. We all have our lives to live and our choices to make alone. You may consult any number of people about your decisions, and get their advice; but no one can make your choices except yourself. You have a life to live, and nobody can live it for you, however much they want to help you, and however much you want to get rid of responsibility.

You have a death to die, and no one can die it for you. Even if you have never in all your life been alone with your own soul, even if you have always lived with the crowd, you can't die like that. 'I shall die alone,' said Pascal. 'Every man,' said Martin Luther, 'must fight his own fight with death. . . . In that hour I may not stand with you, nor you with me.' We must all go out on that last great journey alone. Truly, then, in life and in death every man's soul is his own secret.

(2) *There is One who knows all our secrets.* That is God. Jesus calls Him 'thy Father which is in secret'. That is, He is there when nobody else is there.

Surely what is wrong with a great many lives is that they do not really turn for themselves to that Almighty Father and Friend. It is not that they are hypocrites and pretenders like some of the people Jesus meant. But they try to satisfy themselves with something less intimate than the friendship of God. Even their religion stops short of that. It stops short with mere religious sociability, or with a busy round of good works—all very well, all very friendly and helpful, but it doesn't go very deep, and it has hardly any secret solitary side to it, hardly anything that goes on between the soul and God.

Isn't that true of a great many people? They try, as it were, to get themselves carried on into God's Kingdom in the swim of a merely sociable Christianity, with a human fellowship that doesn't go very deep, and no divine fellowship at all. And they don't want anything more (or they think they don't). They would shrink from anything more intimate and from a divine Friend who would know all their secrets. But all the time their hearts are being starved. Underneath all the sociability there is an unutterable loneliness; because the loneliness of the soul can only be met and cured by the friendship of God. We can't really be satisfied with anything less. It is not enough to have a God of the Church and the crowd and the social family circle, a God who vanishes and leaves our hearts empty when we find ourselves alone.

What we want, even when we shrink from it, is One who knows all our secrets, even our secret sins; One who knows us better than we know ourselves; One of whose presence we can be sure wherever we go, in company or alone, on land or on water, by day or by night, at home amid all the associations of religion or abroad in some environment where we are thrown back on ourselves—as Kipling says: 'East of Suez . . . on the road to Mandalay, where there ain't no Ten Commandments.'

You remember how the ancient Psalmist put it, rejoicing with wonder and awe that he could never get away from God:

O Lord, thou hast searched me and known me. Thou knowest my down-sitting and mine uprising, thou understandest my thought afar off. Thou compassest my path and my lying down and art acquainted with all my ways. For there is not a word in my tongue, but lo, O Lord, thou knowest it altogether. . . . Whither shall I go from thy Spirit? Or whither shall I flee from thy presence? If I ascend up into heaven, thou art there; if I make my bed in the grave, behold thou art there.

The ancient mariner said:

> This soul hath been
> Alone on a wide, wide sea;
> So lonely 'twas that God Himself
> Scarce seemed there to be.

But the Psalmist said:

Search me, O God, and know my heart. Try me, and know my thoughts, and see if there be any wicked way in me. And lead me in the way everlasting.

The man who wrote that lived hundreds of years before the words of our text were spoken by Jesus, but he knew something of 'the Father who dwells in secret'.

And I want to say to you: Don't be content to stop short of that. Don't be content with the kind of religion which is only sociability—the pleasant feeling of a well-lit church on a Sunday evening, or the comfortable sense of being busy with your fellow members in the service of the Church.

All very well, but what would the Church of Christ be in the world if it were made up of people to whom God meant no more than that? And what kind of help is that sort of religion going to give you as you pass through the really difficult places of life? How long will it last amid the hurly-burly of this world? How long will it stand the changes of life? How much of it will be left when you find yourself really alone?

Ah, friends, and especially young men and women, if you are going to have religion at all, let it be the real thing. Of course you must have Christian comradeship with your fellows; but you'll never have it really until you go deep down to find it—deep down to the meeting-place of kindred minds in the knowledge of God.

Make up your mind for that. Stop being content with substitutes. Turn your own heart to God, as your Father and your Friend, the One who knows all your secrets and can cure the loneliness of your heart.

(3) *There is One who can lead us into the secret of God.* That is Jesus Christ. Now that does not come into our text in so many words. It does not mention Jesus. No, but it was

spoken by Jesus; it was He who gave God that name, 'thy Father which is in secret'. And that makes all the difference. For it is Jesus that can lead us into the secret of God.

How much we need that help! The things I have been speaking of are great and high, and perhaps some of us feel that they are too high for us, and we are discouraged. The Father who dwells in secret, the great God whom no man hath seen nor can see, who dwells in unapproachable light, and yet from whose Spirit none can escape away—how far above us it all sounds!

No wonder! The word 'God' is the most profoundly mysterious word in all human speech. How can we pray to Him, unseen and unspeakable? How can we be sure of Him? How are we to conceive or imagine Him? How can we blundering ignorant men and women enter into that secret realm, and come to know God and have Him as our Father and our Friend? We are inclined to cry out, with that same old Psalmist: 'Such knowledge is too wonderful for me: it is high; I cannot attain unto it.'

And what is the answer to that cry?

Well, there is one fact which makes all the difference. Nineteen centuries ago there lived in Palestine One through whom God became plainer and nearer by far than anywhere else in the whole history of the world.

It was the One who spoke the words of our text. It was Jesus, and whenever we feel ourselves lost in the great mysterious realm of religion, whenever we find ourselves floundering in a vain attempt at the knowledge of God—then we come back to Jesus, to the plain story of His life in the Gospels, told by His disciples, and witnessed to by His Church. And when we get there, the mists fall away, we know what God is like—at least we know enough, we know where to find Him. Jesus Christ is the Way, the Truth and the Life. Seeing Him, we see the Father. He can lead us into the secret of God.

How thankful every seeking soul ought to be that the secret of God is an open secret in Jesus!

4. ENTHUSIASM AND COLD WATER

And when the chief priests and scribes saw the wonderful things that he did, and the children crying in the temple, and saying, Hosanna to the son of David; they were sore displeased, and said unto him, Hearest thou what these say? And Jesus saith unto them, Yea; have ye never read, Out of the mouth of babes and sucklings thou hast perfected praise?
MATTHEW 21.15,16

IN this world you nearly always find enthusiasm and criticism side by side. Where you get the enthusiast you usually get the critic and the cynic too.

It is rather notable how you get that time after time in the story of the last week of Jesus' life before the Crucifixion—that week of which the whole Christian world thinks with reverence during the days before Easter. That was indeed a great week in the history of mankind, in which a great drama was being played, the forces of good arrayed against the forces of evil, all sorts of people being unconsciously tested and shown up, the thoughts of many hearts being revealed. And during that week, as it is described in the Gospel pages, time after time you find some revealing incident in which these two types stand out: on the one hand the enthusiast, grasping something of the greatness and majesty of the occasion and pouring out his heart in wonder, love and praise; and on the other hand the inevitable critic, the wet-blanket, with a cold mean kind of common sense and worldly wisdom.

You get it in the house at Bethany. There was the woman who came impulsively with an alabaster cruse of very costly ointment to anoint the head of Jesus in His hour of difficulty and danger. It was a beautiful enthusiastic thing to do. It might be a little difficult to defend it in the cold light of reason. It looks a little extravagant—perhaps we might catch ourselves thinking that. And sure enough there were some there who thought it and said it. 'She shouldn't have done it. That expensive ointment might have fetched a lot of money, for the benefit of the poor.' I don't suppose these were really the people who gave most to the poor themselves. But they were the inevitable critics, the cold-water pourers, the people who had never done a beautiful impulsive thing in their lives; and now they must criticize what the woman had done and so do their best to spoil it.

Well, it wasn't these careful unimaginative people that Jesus agreed with. He agreed with the woman. He liked what she had done. He appreciated it—the beauty of it, the enthusiasm of it.

You get the same two types again in the story of the Triumphal Entry into Jerusalem. We can see now what a very great occasion that was—Jesus the King riding into Jerusalem where He was to be condemned to death. ('In lowly pomp ride on to die.') The people then couldn't quite know all that, but some of them at least had an inkling that something great was happening, and they were greatly moved, and their enthusiasm broke out in shouts. 'Blessed be the kindgom of our father David, that cometh in the name of the Lord. Hosanna in the highest.' But among the crowd there were inevitably some of the other type. The wet-blanket was sure to be there. Some Pharisees were there, and their hearts began to freeze. They frowned and said to Jesus, 'Rabbi, rebuke your disciples.'

And did He? Did Jesus stop the shouting—Jesus who was so humble and unobtrusive? No, He said (and surely the words are full of deep emotion, and of the poetry of emotion): 'I tell you that, if these were to keep silent, the very stones would cry out.' It was a great moment, and there was nothing for it but enthusiasm. According to Jesus it was the cool canny critics who were blind and wrong and the enthusiasts who were right.

Then you get the same thing again in this passage of our text. It was in the Temple, perhaps that same afternoon of Palm Sunday. This time the enthusiasts were children. Jesus was so amazing that those children got infected by the wonder of it, and began shouting, 'Hosanna to the son of David.'

Children do rise to an occasion, and open their hearts and let themselves go. In this case indeed we might be inclined to think it was mere noise and excitement. What could these children really know about it? They had simply caught up the cry they had heard on the lips of older people, and that sort of thing ought to be discouraged. That is perhaps what we would have said if we had been there. And that is just what the priests and scribes did say—the critics, the wise-acres, the wet-blankets. But were they right? Wasn't there more than that in the shouting of the children? Don't you think these children were genuinely captivated by the goodness and charm of Jesus?

And wouldn't Jesus have said that in a sense children are pretty good judges? Of course they have their limitations. But Jesus would have said that in certain ways you have to be like children if you are ever going to be the right sort of men or women. There are certain things you'll never understand so long as you have a cold hard critical mind. You've got to have something of the spontaneity and enthu-siasm of children. There's nothing like it. There's nobody like children for praising God. Or at least there's something in their praising of God that grown-up people need very badly to get back. And so when the children were shouting Hosanna, and the scribes shook their heads and criticized and said protestingly to Jesus, 'Do you hear what these children are saying?' He replied: 'Yes; and have you never read this scripture: Out of the mouth of babes and sucklings hast thou received perfect praise?'

It is a great lesson about enthusiasm and the danger of quenching it. Let us try to apply that lesson.

(1) *Beware of quenching people's enthusiasm.* It is what the scribes and Pharisees apparently did a good deal; as it were, putting their hands on the children's mouths, teaching the children to look askance at Jesus. Could they have done any sadder work?

Children naturally have extraordinarily open trustful generous hearts, uncritical, ungrudging, free from jealousy. They make friends, they accept love, they are blissfully unaware of class-distinctions and barriers, they think no evil, they are enthusiastic. But sometimes they gradually and unconsciously learn another spirit from the grown-up people around them. They hear the older folk talking maliciously, whispering meanly. They get a glimpse of a world of guile and jealousy and snobbery and even trickery, and they conclude that that is the real world. They learn unconsciously the mean secrets of worldly wisdom, cold looks, cold hearts. And how sad that is! Children have necessarily much to learn. But how sad it is when they learn that kind of thing which they need never learn! We ought to be infinitely careful never to do anything by act or word or look or gesture that will help to tarnish the freshness of the enthusiasm of a child.

And it isn't only to the children around us we owe that duty, but to everybody. Don't make it difficult for people to believe in what is great and good and generous. There always are the critics alongside of the enthusiasts. And when critic means wet-blanket, cold-water pourer, cynic, it is a very poor part to play in this world. It is the very opposite of the spirit of Jesus, who never broke the bruised reed or quenched the smouldering wick, who welcomed the enthusiasm of those children shouting Hosanna. Beware of quenching people's enthusiasm.

(2) *Beware of letting your own enthusiasm be quenched.* That does often happen with the passing years. There is no doubt whatever that Jesus saw in children something delightful which often passes away, but which grown-up people must get back if they've lost it: a simplicity, spontaneity, gaiety, generosity, enthusiasm; and it gets dulled and stiffened, so often, as we go through life. Tom Hood wrote very sadly,

> Now 'tis little joy
> To know I'm farther off from Heaven
> Than when I was a boy.

Poor sad Lord Byron wasn't very old when he wrote:

> There's not a joy the world can give like that it takes away,
> When the glow of early thought declines in feeling's dull decay.
> 'Tis not on youth's smooth cheek alone the blush that fades so fast,
> But the tender bloom of heart is gone ere youth itself be past.

It is a case of letting the heart grow old and stiff and dull and earthly instead of keeping it fresh and young, generous and enthusiastic. Sometimes it is one thing, sometimes it is another, that does the damage—jealousy, pride, discontent. Perhaps oftenest of all it is the obsession with material things, what Tennyson calls 'the narrowing lust of gold'. It does narrow a man's soul.

And there is many a man who in his youth was capable of generous enthusiasms and idealisms, but who got caught up in the love of material prosperity and success, and his heart stiffened and narrowed, and now he couldn't shout 'Hosanna' to save his life, and he is much more careful about his enthusiasms—he won't inconvenience himself much now for the high Christian causes he once cared for—he is too much a man of the world for that. But that is one of the saddest things in the world. Listen to this sentence: 'All

other faults or deficiencies Christ could tolerate, but he could
have neither part nor lot with men destitute of enthusiasm.'

You, young men and women, if you are going to be
Christians at all, as you profess to be, don't let yourselves
have the safe conventional kind of Christianity that never
runs away with you. You men and women who are growing
into middle age, don't let yourselves become middle aged in
the dull sort of way which means just losing your
enthusiasms.

That need never happen. Surely it won't happen to those
who have in them the real religion of Jesus, faith and hope
and love and the spirit of service and sacrifice. To those who
have that spirit life will always be an adventure. It will be
wonderful, and it will grow more and more wonderful, and
you will more and more want to lift up your heart in
Hosannas of wonder, love and praise.

(3) There is one particular enthusiasm still to be mentioned: *the enthusiasm for the missionary enterprise of the Church
of Christ.*

I said that wherever the enthusiast is to be found the critic
is sure to be found too. There could hardly be a better
example of that than the missionary enterprise. It is a magnificent enthusiasm. But it always has its critics, its wet-
blankets, its cold-water pourers, the people who don't believe
in missions, and who shake their heads and shrug their
shoulders—just like the critics over and over again in the
Gospel story.

Perhaps it is no wonder. The missionary enterprise is such
a big thing. It is such a mad thing. St. Paul himself, talking
of that mad enterprise of his, to try to conquer the Roman
Empire and the world with a queer new message about a
man who had been crucified, called it 'the foolishness of
preaching'. It looked like a mad sort of thing.

It is told of the Spanish Saint Theresa in the sixteenth

century that one day when she was ten years old she set off with her little brother to convert the Moors to Christianity! What a charming childish dream! And this whole business of Foreign Missions looks like a charming childish dream, a bit of madness, 'the foolishness of the Evangel'.

Yes—but Paul went on to say that if it was foolishness it was a divine kind of foolishness, and that the foolishness of God is wiser than men. And of course he was right—it was he and his comrades that were really doing something worth while amid the chaos of that ancient world. And as for the charming childish dream—well, Jesus would say, as He said to the cold critics that day in the Temple, 'Have you never read the text, "Out of the mouths of babes and sucklings thou hast perfected praise"?' The enthusiasts were right.

In the modern world too the enthusiasts are right. As for the kind of Christianity that is going to keep itself to itself, with a charity that begins at home and stops at home, safe and conventional, stiffened up in its Sunday best, parochial and unimaginative, as if Scotland were the whole world— that kind of thing is simply a back number in the modern world, Rip van Winkle lost in a new age. Every decent Sunday School has got beyond that outlook before now. That kind of Christianity has no future. Either Christianity is going to die, or it is going to rejuvenate the whole world. And if it isn't going to rejuvenate the whole world, I don't know what is. There are many enterprises in this world about which it really is not worth while to be enthusiastic. But if there is one thing in this modern world that is really worth doing, worth getting enthusiastic about, it is what is being done by the Church's missionaries.

Friends, if the Gospel is true, it is a very big thing indeed. You and I believe it is true. We even sing Hosanna about it. Then let us treat it as a big thing—give it room in our lives, give it room in the world and say every day with heart and life and voice: 'Blessed is the Kingdom that cometh in the name of the Lord.'

5. PRAYER FOR WISDOM

If any of you lack wisdom, let him ask of God, that giveth to all men liberally, and upbraideth not; and it shall be given him. But let him ask in faith, nothing wavering. JAMES 1.5, 6

WHEN James wrote these words, I wonder if he was thinking at all of the old story of how Solomon felt he lacked wisdom for his great task, and asked God for it, and got it. The story illustrates exactly what James meant when he said: 'If any of you lack wisdom, let him ask of God.' There was young Solomon, called to the throne when he was a mere lad. And in his dream he prayed: 'O Lord, my God, thou hast made thy servant king in place of David my father; and I am but a little child: I know not how to go out or come in. Give therefore thy servant an understanding heart to judge thy people, that I may discern between good and bad.' James was not writing to kings in this letter, but to very ordinary people for the most part. Yet even among them, with their more commonplace tasks, there would surely be some who needed wisdom and wished they had more of it. For everybody has some responsibilities and all except the very foolish wish sometimes that they had more wisdom.

We don't go very far in this our human life without coming to find ourselves in such situations. We find life becoming complicated, with problems to face, and decisions to be made, and sides to take, and tasks to discharge. We may take counsel with our friends, but after all we have to bear the responsibilities ourselves. And don't we sometimes find ourselves wishing we had more wisdom?

You can think for yourselves of the different kinds of

responsibilities I mean. Some people have them in public life, in the service of the community or the Church, where it is often difficult to know how to act for the best. Some people have them in the private life of the home, especially, for example, parents who have the task of bringing up children, surely one of the most difficult and responsible tasks in the world, constantly requiring wisdom.

As regards our own personal lives, we all at one time or another have difficult decisions to make. And all these things are quite especially true in these testing days of ours. What thoughts ought we to be thinking about the present and the future of our Western civilization? And what ought we to do at this point and at that: Where does our duty lie? So many of the ordinary safe rules about the conduct of life become inadequate and we find ourselves wishing that we had, as Solomon put it, more 'understanding to discern between good and bad'. 'If any of you lack wisdom,' says James. Well, that is just what we do feel we lack, and need more of it—just wisdom.

How can we get it? There is hardly anything more difficult to get. We can't get it from books alone, though they can teach us many things. Wisdom is a different thing from learning, and it does not always go with learning. It comes only in the experience of life, and sometimes at the cost of many blunders and failures. Is there then any way of avoiding these blunders and failures, and getting wisdom when we need it? Is there any secret, any sure and simple way for us ordinary men and women who so often feel that we need more widsom than we have?

This text says Yes. 'If any of you lack wisdom, let him ask of God, who gives to all men liberally and without reproach, and it shall be given him. Only, let him ask in faith, nothing doubting.' That text tells us very plainly of a method of getting wisdom, and of a condition that is attached, and I want to speak now of the method and the condition. We may learn a good deal not only about wisdom, but about the whole life of religion.

(1) *The method.* It can be stated in a very few words. It amounts to this: just asking God, praying to God. 'If any of you lacks wisdom, let him ask of God.' Is it too simple to be real? Is it too good to be true? In this world there are many ways of getting what we want. But is this a real way—the method of just asking for it?

The New Testament is certainly full of that method. There is no mistake about it. Jesus said: 'Ask, and it shall be given you.' 'If you who are evil know how to give good gifts to your children, how much more will your Heavenly Father give good things to those who ask Him.'

And throughout the New Testament you find the followers of Jesus quite convinced that prayer is a real thing, that can make a difference. But is it? Some people will tell you that it is simply a bit of old superstition—this idea of getting a thing by praying for it. In African tribes the witch-doctor tries to bring on rain in the midst of drought by his incantations, or to cure sickness by some ritual instead of by some medicine. And some people will tell you that all prayer is on a level with that, a mere relic of old superstitious ideas—as if praying for a thing could make any difference. And perhaps many others who wouldn't say that do unconsciously think something like that in their hearts, and that is why they pray so little.

I do not say that we ought to pray for rain when we happen to want it, or that we ought even to think of prayer as a quick and easy way of getting everything we would like. That would not give us a very worthy idea of God or of religion. But let us take this case of wisdom and see how the method works. Think of some cases.

Imagine the case of a great statesman in a time of grave

35

crisis, preparing for a meeting of his cabinet at which a supremely important decision has to be made. Then, if ever, a man would require wisdom, and almost any man would wish he had more of it. Suppose that this man is not only a great statesman, but also a profoundly religious and Christian man (as some of our great British statesmen have been). And suppose that in the days when he is looking forward to his fateful cabinet meeting he has recourse to prayer. Suppose that he steeps himself in the atmosphere of prayer and the presence of God before he goes to his meeting, and really seeks the light of God upon his problems—in fact, asks God for wisdom. What will be the result? Will it not be that when the occasion comes, he will be ready for it? And as he presides over the turmoil of a dissentient cabinet, his soul will be calmed by the peace of God, his courage will be high, his vision will be clear, his mind will be raised above the fog of personal fears and grudges. In fact, his mind will be breathing calm and heavenly wisdom, 'the widsom that is from above, which (as this Epistle says) is first pure, then peaceable, gentle, and easy to be entreated, full of mercy and good fruits, without partiality, and without hypocrisy.' The man who had asked for wisdom would get it from God.

You may imagine any number of cases: an employer of labour dealing with an industrial dispute, a mother dealing with some specially difficult problem in bringing up her children, a congregation choosing a new minister. Can't you see how in all such cases prayer is a real secret—not as a magic way of consulting an oracle, but as a channel through which God's wisdom may come into human hearts?

But, instead of imagining cases, let me give you a case from the history of our country. It is from the story of the Westminster Assembly, that great assembly of divines in the seventeenth century which drew up our Confession of Faith and our Shorter Catechism. At that assembly the leader of the Erastian party was Dr John Selden, one of the greatest scholars in Christendom. After he had set forth and championed the Erastian heresy, the good Presbyterians were very much at a loss as to how to defend the truth against that brilliant argument for Erastianism. Then unexpectedly there rose up in the meeting a saintly young Scotsman, George Gillespie, one of the youngest members of the whole Assembly, and spoke for an hour against the heresy in a most extraordinarily effective way, in a speech which Dr Selden afterwards admitted had swept away the work of ten years of his life. When Gillespie's inspired speech was over, his friends got hold of the notebook that had lain in front of him, hoping to find the outline of his argument. But on the page they found nothing but one little sentence, pencilled over and over again as he sat there waiting to speak—just these three Latin words: Da lucem, Domine, 'Give light, O Lord.'

That is a classical instance of how prayer can be a real method of getting wisdom.

(2) But to make the truth still plainer, note that there is a *condition* attached. 'If any of you lack wisdom, let him ask of God . . . and it will be given him. Only, let him ask in faith, nothing wavering (nothing doubting).'

You see what that means. It means that, if you are to get this heavenly wisdom, you must be prepared really to trust it and follow it. You must open your heart honestly and singly to it, without hesitancy, without compromising. It will not do to trust half to the wisdom you are praying for and half to shifty and worldly devices. If you pray for guidance in that spirit, of course it will not come. It can't, because you are not really looking for it and are not prepared to take it when it comes.

How clearly that comes out in James's words! 'Let him ask in faith, nothing doubting. For he that doubteth is like the surge of the sea, driven and tossed by the wind. Let not that man think that he shall receive anything from the Lord —double-minded man that he is, unstable in all his ways.'

Why doesn't such a man get the wisdom he is asking for? Because he is not really asking for it with all his heart: he doesn't mean to follow it unless it suits his own plans. He is thinking perhaps too much of his own convenience and credit and triumph, and is really trusting to earthly wisdom though he is praying for heavenly wisdom. He is double-minded and real wisdom doesn't come because he hasn't fulfilled the condition.

How true that is! And how right this condition is! And all this makes us think finally of how much Christian faith and devotion can do to enrich and ennoble the most ordinary lives—lives that seem to lack distinction and capacity—lives that lack wisdom. If they truly turn to God, He will make them wise. For, as James puts it, God gives to all men liberally and without upbraiding, if they really seek. He does not despise the ordinary and blundering people. He is not impatient of them. He will not upbraid or reproach them for being commonplace. He will not give a stone if they ask for bread, or a rebuff if they ask for wisdom. He will make them wise.

It is the very glory of the Christian religion that it is for all sorts and conditions of ordinary men who will accept it. So it has been through the whole history of the Christian Church. So it has been quite notably in our own land of Scotland. Ordinary men and women, the rank and file of humanity, from castle to cottage, up and down our land, have learnt this secret, and by simple faith and prayer have become wise unto salvation, and wise for the service of God and man. Therefore, 'if any of you lack wisdom, let him ask of God.' How different this secret is from a magical way of getting what we want, and how deeply based on the spiritual laws of God's universe! That is the way the universe is built, so that many a man, trying to be wise and clever for his own glory or convenience, never learns real wisdom; while many another, very conscious of his lack of wisdom for his responsibilities, does grow wonderfully wise, with the best kind of wisdom, because he seeks it with a simple and honest heart.

Jesus once rejoiced and said: 'I thank Thee, O Father, Lord of heaven and earth, that thou hast concealed these things from the wise and prudent, and hast revealed them unto babes. Even so, Father, for so it seemed good in thy sight.'

He does not despise commonplace and blundering people. He is not impatient with them. He does not upbraid or reproach them when they turn to Him for the wisdom they lack—if only they ask with honest and believing hearts.

D

6. GOD IN CHRIST AND GOD IN OUR FELLOW CREATURES

No man hath seen God at any time; the only begotten Son, which is in the bosom of the Father, he hath declared him.   St. John 1.18

No man hath seen God at any time. If we love one another, God dwelleth in us, and his love is perfected in us.   1 John 4.12

THE man who wrote these two sentences that begin so similarly, at different times, may be regarded as one of the great mystics of the New Testament. We are all familiar with his mystical way of writing. Mysticism in religion is a thing which is easier to recognize than to define. But we all have a rough idea of what it means. The mystic is a man who claims to see the unseen world in a direct way of his own. He tries to get beyond all mists and barriers into the very being of God Himself—beyond all words and thoughts, beyond all human aims and interests, into a realm where he loses himself in the vision of God.

You think that sounds terribly airy and unpractical. Of course it does. The mystical way of religion has often been criticized on just these grounds. The mystic seems to lose touch with earth and reality. He seems to lose touch with history, with the plain story of God's historical revelation to men, and he flies off into the clouds of abstraction to find God in some original way for himself.

For another thing, the mystic sometimes seems to forget that he is living in a world of men and women, and he becomes self-centred and unpractical in his religion. These are the things that have often made people suspicious of what is called mysticism.

But what strikes me as I read these two sentences from

John (whoever he was) is that, mystic or no mystic, he is extraordinarily sane and practical, and also extraordinarily helpful and encouraging to people who are perplexed about the mysteries of God and religion. If he is a mystic, he is also an extraordinarily level-headed person, and he emphasizes the very two things that mysticism is often supposed to forget.

This mystic does not get lost in the mysteries of the divine nature, does not get so blinded by a vision of God that he can't see his fellow creatures. No, he tells us plainly that in this life there is no immediate vision of God: 'No man has seen God at any time.'

And then he tells us how after all we *can* get into touch with God and be sure of Him, not by any imaginations, but in simple practical ways. In the one text he is thinking of one way, and in the other he is thinking of another, though really they both go together. And these are the two: we can get to God through Jesus Christ, and we can get to God by brotherly love. These are the two guiding stars that are to keep us right as regards the God whom we cannot see. So John tells us in these two books. In his Gospel it is: 'No man has ever seen God; but the only begotten Son who is in the bosom of the Father, he has declared him.' And in the Epistle: 'No man has ever seen God; but if we love one another, God dwells in us and his love is perfected in us.'

That is to say: there is no direct vision of God; but there is the Gospel story of Jesus for our illumination, and there are our fellow creatures to be loved and served; and that is where God is. These are the two poles of Christian mysticism or, we may say, of the Christian religion: God in Christ and God in our fellow creatures. Let us think what that means.

(1) *God in Christ.* The word 'God' is more surrounded by mystery than any other word in all human speech—the

mystery that John means when he says 'No man has ever seen God'. Therefore in every age and in every place, but especially in the haunts of youth, there are people who are in perplexity about God.

With some of you it may be perplexity as regards belief. You have found yourself, even against your will, doubting the things you have been taught to believe. You don't want to doubt, you want to believe, but you find yourself asking miserably: How can I be sure? How can I know that there is a reality corresponding to the word 'God'? You are in 'the valley of the shadow of doubt'.

To others of you who are differently built, the perplexity comes in a different way—less intellectual, more practical. You may not have actual doubts about the whole truth of religion, but you find it hard to make God real. You can't pray to Him with any sense of reality. I think everybody who has ever really tried to pray must have felt that difficulty. We are speaking to a mysterious Being whom we can't see. How are we to imagine or conceive Him as we approach Him? What is God like? Sometimes perhaps we think of Him in a very familiar way, like a human friend. And then we feel that is too human, too petty. And so next our imaginations put Him far off, sublime, awful, incomprehensible. And then again that seems too cold and distant.

So there is all that floundering and uncertainty in our thought of God. How can we get away from it? How can we ever feel sure we have a grasp of God as He really is, and that our prayers are really reaching the great Being whom no man has ever seen? I am sure some of you have sometimes felt these perplexities and perhaps feel them now. What can I say to you?

I want to remind you that you and I are not the first who have tried to pray to God. We are not lonely pioneers making our way across a trackless desert. We have a long and precious tradition of religion behind us to point the way and to set us right. It began for most of us at our mother's knee, but it stretches back through unnumbered generations of men and women who sought and found God. And it goes back above all and through all to the great Revealer of God, Jesus Christ, to whom all these other witnesses are but guiding stars like the star in the story of Epiphany. Jesus Christ can set us right. He can make us feel sure.

Now that is just what John is telling us, in his own way, in this first text: that amid all the mystery somehow the very nature of God becomes manifest through Jesus Christ. 'No man has ever seen God; but the only begotten Son, who is in the bosom of the Father, he has declared him (or interpreted him).' There John is referring to a plain fact of history, a thing that was seen on this earth of ours, a thing which (as he says) men's eyes had beheld and their hands had handled—a human life which had been lived among men, the life of Jesus of Nazareth.

That is what we Christians always come back to—God is a great mystery, and our minds flounder about in thought and prayer, not knowing how to conceive or realize Him, tossed about by perplexed and shifting imaginations. But then we bring our minds back to Jesus Christ, how He spoke of God, how He prayed to God, how wherever He went He helped men to believe in the God He believed in, and His very presence made men see what God was really like, until their deepest instincts told them it was true.

We come back to that; and as we get into that atmosphere of the Gospel story, illuminated by the age-long witness of Christ's people, as we stand beside Jesus and see things from that angle, then we too begin to be sure that we are seeing God as He really is—the God and Father of our Lord Jesus Christ.

'No man has ever seen God'—the uncreated unbegotten

eternal God; but somehow we can see God incarnate, God only-begotten, the only-begotten Son, as John puts it. Seeing Jesus Christ, we do somehow see the Father; and that is the guiding star of the Christian mystic—God in Christ.

(2) *God in our fellow creatures.* That is of course in a different sense. But that is the other way in which this great mystic teaches us to realize God. He points us to our fellow creatures and tells us to love them. 'No man has ever seen God; but if we love one another, God dwells in us and his love is perfected in us.' God is mysterious, ineffable, incomprehensible. How then can we make sure of Him and love Him and serve Him? Well, says John, if we want to do that, we must find Him in our fellow creatures and love and serve them. Do mystics sometimes forget that they are living in a world of men and women? Do they become self-centred with their visions of God? Not this one. For he says: we can't see God, but we can see men, and it is when we love and serve men that our love for God is the real thing.

It is quite extraordinary how this great mystic, over and over again in his little Epistle, brings down all divine mysteries to this practical test, and bids us love God in our fellow creatures. 'God is love, and he that dwells in love dwells in God and God in him.' 'He that loveth not his brother whom he hath seen, how can he love God whom he hath not seen?' 'He that loveth his brother dwelleth in the light.'

John speaks as if this were not only the test, but even the very essence of loving God—to love one's fellow creatures in daily life. We can't see God, we can't do Him any good directly, we can't pour out our love in any strange mystical ways on Him. But we can love our fellows. We can stand by them. They need it. And that is what God wants.

We might almost dare to put it: God does not want our love for Himself, He only wants it for other men and women whom we can serve and help. Or rather, God wants us in that sense to find Him in our fellows, and by loving them to love Him.

That is where we touch reality. And religious emotion needs that kind of test. For some people it is quite easy to feel religious emotions and to take pleasure in them, to be agreeably moved by prayers and hymns, because they have been brought up amid such associations. But some outsider might ask, What is the good of all that? He might tell us that it is just one form of excitement, and that, while we take our excitement in that form, others prefer to take it in what we call secular forms, and it is just as good. All this mysterious traffic that we call religion—what is the good of it? Where does it touch reality? And I don't see how we can ever answer that question unless our lives are showing that our religion is drawing us nearer to our fellow creatures in love and loyalty, keeping our personal relationships right in this workaday world.

If it is not doing that, then not only the outsider but this John himself would be profoundly suspicious of it. To talk about loving and serving God—that may be mere phantasy or stuffy sentimentality. The testing question is: Does our love for God express itself in our daily personal relationships, in brave loyal unselfish living among our fellows? If not, it never gets anywhere near the real God at all.

Now that is a testing truth for those of us who profess to be Christians. But it can also be a wonderfully illuminating truth to those who are a little mystified about religion. You know that you are called to love God with your whole heart, and perhaps you sometimes wonder whether you love Him at all, and how you can, and how you are to make sure, since He is so surrounded by mystery. There are many mysteries in religion, but there are many plain things too, and the plainest of all is the daily opportunity of standing by our fellow creatures according to the brave rule of brotherly love. We may be perplexed about many things, but there we can't go wrong or stumble. And isn't that enough to go on with? A star to follow?

I have been trying to speak especially to those who are perplexed about God. I began by pointing you to Jesus Christ, and that is both the beginning and the end, for all that I have said about the plain path of brotherly love—that belongs to Christ too. And if at first in your doubt and perplexity you cannot see any more of the light of Christ than that, you can at least see that and follow it.

We all know the beautiful story of the wise men following the star. But haven't you heard the new chapter that medieval legend added to the story—the legend of the other wise man, who could not follow the star with his companions because he was called aside by a simple duty of human kindness and mercy to a fellow creature, which cost him his life? He never came to the manger at Bethlehem, but he did not miss the Christ, for Christ was revealed to him in a vision, just where he was, before he died. Brotherly love was his guiding star, and it was the light of Christ.

My brother, it may be that you, in your perplexity, cannot yet see God in Christ, and so you are not satisfied. It is a good thing that you are not satisfied. But you can at least see enough of the light of Christ to follow, in a brave loyal unselfish life among your fellows.

Yes, in that sense you too can follow Christ. And the rest will come. He that followeth Christ, even in perplexity, shall not walk in darkness, but shall have the light of life.

7. THE CHURCH OF THE LIVING GOD

The church of the living God, the pillar and ground of the truth.
1 TIMOTHY 3.15

THERE is no doubt that St. Paul was a high-churchman, in the best sense of the term. That is, he believed with all his heart in the Church of Christ as an essential part of the Gospel. There are many good people who do not. And I am not thinking of the outsiders. Of course, there are many religious outsiders, who say: 'Religion, yes; Christianity, yes; but Church no.' But I am not thinking of these. I am thinking of the churchgoers who do not very deeply believe in the Church, or at least not very enthusiastically. We have become so accustomed nowadays to sighing and shaking our heads over the Church—its failures, its imperfections, its problems, its uncertain prospects. The very word has become a dull word for many of us, and nobody expects anything but a dull sermon on such a subject.

What a contrast to the apostle Paul! He believed with all his heart in the Church. There was far less to show for it then than there is today. The numbers were very small, though they were growing rapidly. It had no buildings at all. It had no worldly prestige. It didn't pay then to be a Church member, it was a disadvantage. Yet a man like St. Paul could speak of the Church with the eager kind of devotion you might find in a keen midshipman telling of his ship, or a born soldier telling of his regiment, only much more and deeper. A warmth comes into his tones, and his language becomes like poetry when he mentions the word.

It is good for us to stir up our minds to think of the Church like that. So I take as our text those great words:

47

'the Church of the living God, the pillar and ground of the truth.'

This text, with its two separate phrases, suggests that the Church is both a stable thing to rest on and a moving thing to follow. It is a pillar, with its base firmly planted in the soil of the past, 'the pillar and ground of the truth'. But it is also a living and moving thing, 'the Church of the living God', advancing into the future, with the life and power of God Himself, like the pillar of cloud by day and of fire by night that led the Israelites forward through the wilderness in the old story. Let us think for a little of these two aspects of it, taking the two phrases of the text in reverse order for convenience' sake.

(1) *The pillar and ground of the truth.* What a solid and reassuring phrase that is amid the uncertainties of the world! But we must ask, what does it mean?

Does it mean that, while everything is uncertain, you and I are to accept the doctrines of Christianity blindly just because the Church asserts them; that we must believe in God and Christ and the Atonement simply because the Church says so? Does it mean that we can't expect to know anything about these matters for ourselves, and that we must base them simply on the authority of the Church, which is 'the pillar and ground of the truth'?

Surely not. Surely Christianity doesn't ask us to shut our eyes and be spoon fed, and take everything on trust at second hand. That is not how Jesus dealt with men or with truth. Martin Luther in a famous passage tells us of a peasant who was asked one day by a stranger he met in the forest what he believed in the way of religion. He replied, 'What the Church believes,' and that was all he could say. Luther goes on to declare in the strongest language that such a man can't possibly be saved. Luther meant that a Christian must know for himself what be believes, and be able to give a reason for the hope that is in him, with an inward personal faith, the witness of the Holy Spirit in his own individual heart. And Luther was quite right.

And yet (this is what I've been coming to)—what a blessed thing it is that we don't have to stand each one alone in cold and lonely isolation. What a good thing it is that we have the testimony and fellowship of the Church, to encourage our weak faith. What a good thing it is to remember that when we begin to live the Christian life we are not the first, that we are not blazing a new trail for ourselves in an unexplored virgin forest, but have inherited all the experience of nineteen centuries of Christian living and thinking and believing. We have all that behind us, and when we are weary and doubtful we can lean back on that.

In the Life of Temple Gairdner of Cairo, there is a deeply interesting passage, written by him in a letter amid the acute difficulties of his missionary work in Egypt. 'We're not the first to cope with this. The men who really had a hard time were the people in the first centuries when there was no Church History. We have only to look up the Early Fathers to see that our troubles have been survived before. Blessed be God for History.'

Yes, indeed. In that sense we have far more cause than the apostle Paul to rejoice in the Church as 'the pillar and ground of the truth'—because we have behind us nineteen centuries of it, generations of believing men and women of every tribe and tongue and people and nation, witnessing to the truth of the Gospel and handing it down to us. Blessed be God for that.

And blessed be God also for the corporate witness and fellowship of the Church in our own lives today. We do not stand each one alone. We have a great company of believing people, 'one Lord, one faith, one baptism, one God and Father of all'.

A cousin of mine once said to me in a letter: 'I am so glad that I have some relations, because I know some people who haven't any—brothers or sisters or cousins—and it makes such a difference to have them.' Well, it makes such a difference also to have spiritual relations; and shouldn't we be thankful that the Church of Christ gives them to us—all those fathers and mothers and brothers and sisters and friends that Christ promised to His followers?

I remember once at the close of a great religious Congress, when we who were present were feeling tremendously uplifted by the testimony and fellowship of the vast gathering, a friend said to me late on that last night: 'What a good thing it is to have a memory like this to lean back on, in days to come, whenever we are tired and discouraged.' Many of you must have felt the same thing on some special occasion of that sort. But the Church of Christ is always with us, and it ought to be doing that kind of thing for us all the time.

I think we are realizing now especially how important that is for the religion of young souls growing up among us, boys and girls, lads and lasses coming into maturity. We want them to be initiated into the Christian secret as they grow up; we want them to see and know for themselves the truth as it is in Jesus. But that kind of truth can't altogether be put down in black and white on paper and handed out cut-and-dried to each customer. It is in the Church that the truth is enshrined; in the living worship and fellowship of the Christian Society, including all the long discipline from Baptism and Cradle-Roll through Primary Department and Sunday School and Bible Class to the Communion Table; and then, ever after, all the rich fellowship, in work and worship, of a Christian congregation. That is how children grow up into Christian men and women; and that is how we all become built up in Christian faith and life.

How thankful we ought to be for all that! And how these reflections should make us resolve, more convincedly and eagerly than ever, to let our Church be what it ought to be—a great supernatural fellowship in the succession of the apostles and the saints, that can be to us and to our children after us 'the pillar and ground of the truth' in our daily endeavours after the Christian life. May all our Churches be like that!

But that brings us to the other phrase used in our text as a description of the Church.

(2) *The Church of the Living God*. That is the other side of it. It is not only the pillar and ground of the truth, something solid on which we can lean back, something ancestral, inheriting a great tradition from the venerable past. It is also the Church of the Living God, active in the present, and marching forward into the unknown future for all sorts of new adventures. Certainly that was true of the Church of New Testament times. And surely that is important for the Church of our time. You and I are certainly living in an age in which the future is 'all unknown': perhaps the one thing we know about it is that it is going to be very different from the familiar past in many ways.

Prophets like H. G. Wells used to try to portray for us 'the shape of things to come'. They did not agree with each other, but they were all agreed that the old familiar nineteenth century world was gone forever, and that we stand at the end of an era. We have often been inclined to dismiss such sweeping prophecies as mere 'hot air'—we who live in 'this blessed plot of earth', this sheltered island of ours. Convulsive things might happen in other countries, but not in this favoured country, so we thought. But now we can't close our eyes any longer to the changes in world civilization —social, industrial, political, moral and religious changes. There are new tides all over the world just now, and we can no longer believe that these tides are not going to touch our island shores. The change is already going on in our land under our eyes, and as we look back over twenty-five or thirty years we know that now we are living in a different world, and the future is unknown.

As we look into that uncertain future, what are we of the Church of Christ to make of it? I'll tell you what we are apt to do: to tremble for the ark of God, and then proceed to dig ourselves in where we are, or perhaps bury our heads in the sand.

We admit that the prospects of the Church do not look very bright compared with the brave days of old, and we seem sometimes to accept the fact as if it were inevitable, without allowing ourselves to think very much about it. We seem sometimes to regard the Church as a leaking ship, which is bound to founder sooner or later; but meanwhile we'll carry on in the good old way, and try to keep her bows above water a little longer—try to make her last our time at least, though we can't expect to see her touching the wonderful records she made when she was young. Isn't that how we sometimes catch ourselves half unconsciously thinking about—the Church of Christ?

There is a story (often told) of one of the Popes, who was one day standing with a Cardinal inside the gates of the Vatican watching wagons of treasure pass into the grounds for the Papal treasury. The Cardinal, thinking of the story in the Acts, of Peter and John and the lame beggar, said complacently: 'The time is past, Holy Father, when the Church could say, "Silver and gold have I none".' The Pope wisely and sadly replied: 'Past also is the time when the Church could say to a lame man, "In the name of Jesus rise up and walk".'

How a story like that ought to make us think. Is that really the truth about the Church? Is that what we believe about it? That its best days are past, that it will never again do the great things it used to do? I don't mean simply faith-healing, like the cure of that lame man, though that is worth thinking of, but all the magnificent things the Church used to do in the days of Peter and John and Paul. It was then a small and poor and persecuted Church, but it turned the world upside down for Christ, crusading over land and sea for the salvation of mankind, and going on from strength to strength in the power of the Living God. Is all that never going to happen again? Are the Church's great days really past? And if so, why?

Is it because the Gospel is not true? Do we really believe in the Gospel? Are we sure of it? If we are sure of it, if it is really true, if the God who was incarnate in Jesus Christ is still the Living God—then why shouldn't we expect Him, amid all the difficulties of the twentieth century, to do through the Church and the Gospel in this land and every land as great things as have ever been seen before?

And as for the changes that intimidate us when we look into the future, why shouldn't we go out to meet them expecting them to 'prepare in the wilderness a high-way for our God'? Why not—if we really believe in the Gospel?

It all comes back to this in the end: Do we really believe in the Gospel? Yes, it all comes back to what I began with: that we must, each one for himself, as well as altogether, come to know the truth as it is in Jesus. There is no room now for a conventional somnolent Christianity. It must be neck or nothing.

The Church of the Living God must consist of men and women who have a living faith. Its young men and women must be continually growing up into that living experience. We must all make sure for ourselves that we have part and lot in that supernatural fellowship, the Church of the Living

God. And then, come what may, change what may, we shall 'expect great things from God, and attempt great things for Him'.

8. PRIDE AND THE GRACE OF GOD

Not I, but the grace of God which was with me. 1 CORINTHIANS 15.10

IN one of Robert Louis Stevenson's stories there is an incident which we may take as starting-point. Two men are standing together on the shore, beside a lagoon where pearl-fishing is being carried on, and on the beach in front of them lies a diving-costume. The sight of it sets one of them thinking and moralizing, and he makes a parable.

There is the diving-costume designed to cover a man from head to foot as he goes down into the water. It comes up out of the sea, dripping with water, and goes down again, and comes up again dripping with water, and all the while the man inside is untouched—as dry as if he had remained on land.

Well, says the one man, can't we imagine some spiritual kind of dress in which men could go out into the world, and amid all the disturbing and painful influences of life their hearts would remain safe and unharmed, like the man in the diving-costume? Can't we imagine such a dress for the soul?

'Yes,' says the second man, 'it is called self-conceit.' 'Oh,' said the other, 'why not call it the grace of God?'

It is a good parable. There are these two different kinds of armour by which different men contrive to keep themselves unhurt and so manage to go safely through all life's experiences. Some manage it by the armour of conceit, others by the armour of the grace of God. St. Paul managed it by the latter method. And that is precisely expressed in the words of our text, where St. Paul, speaking of his conversion to Christianity and his pioneering work for Christ, says 'Yet not I, but the grace of God which was with me'.

55

St. Paul had a very adventurous life, with many difficult things to do, and many wounds to face. But the most difficult thing he ever had to do was when he had to face up to Christianity, which he had been persecuting, and admit that he had been utterly and dreadfully wrong, and turn round and begin all over again and become a Christian. That is what he has been talking of in these verses—how he must be always the least of the apostles, because he was the last of them; he had been on the wrong side and then had come right, like one born out of due season.

How hard it must have been for his pride—or at least it would have been if he had tried to cling to his pride. He was such a well-known man, a learned man, a Pharisee, a brilliant young fellow, so sure of his convictions, and the pride of his sect. When he was confronted with this new movement called Christianity, it was a great shock—he had to make up his mind about it, and he made up his mind against it and tried to stamp it out. But somehow he couldn't get away from it—it continued to prick his conscience.

If he had determined to stick to his pride, he might have remained a Pharisee to the end of his days, protected against this new disturbing influence by the armour of conceit. But Paul couldn't do that, and so there came the great day on the Damascus road, when Paul had a vision of Christ, and threw his pride to the winds, and turned his back on all he had lived for, and began again at the very beginning as a Christian. And not a sad ashamed kind of Christian either, with pride fallen and conceit broken, and therefore going softly for the rest of his days. No, but a keen bold ardent adventurous enterprising Christian, always in the forefront of the battle, and with head erect, in spite of his long mistake. It was because he had given up the armour of conceit for the armour of the grace of God.

So in this place, after talking of himself as the least and

last of the apostles, he goes on quite serenely. 'But by the grace of God I am what I am. And his grace bestowed on me was not in vain, for I laboured more abundantly than all of them. Yet not I, but the grace of God which was with me.' Not conceit, but the grace of God.

Let us look at those two different kinds of armour.

(1) *The armour of conceit.* Why was it that, while Paul the Pharisee became a Christian, so many other Pharisees remained where they were, high and dry, uninfluenced by Christianity, untouched, unwounded, unblessed? Wasn't it because they were encased in the armour of conceit? That was what kept them safe. Not all of them, surely. It wouldn't be fair to condemn all of them in that way. But many of them—many of the Pharisees whom Jesus encountered. Wasn't that one of the things He saw in them— pride, self-righteousness, self-esteem? They were encased in that armour. When Jesus appeared among them, with His message and His challenge, that was something new and disturbing. And they couldn't bear to be disturbed. They didn't want new truth to upset their little system of things. They didn't want the challenge of a new ethic. They didn't want to have to change their minds about anything, or to be brought to repentance for anything, or to make new resolutions about anything. So they kept themselves safe, high and dry, within their armour of conceit and complacence (like the man in the diving-costume), and nothing could get through it. It kept them safe, sure enough; but it was a deadly kind of safety, for it meant that they never learnt anything, and they got nothing from Christ.

It is quite a common thing still for people to wear the unwholesome kind of armour as they go about the world. For example, there are people who learn very little as they go about the world because they are too proud to admit that they don't know. I dare say most of us are tempted in that direction. We are sometimes too proud to ask questions. Children will always ask them, but we outgrow that, and we pretend to know, and so we don't learn anything like as much as we might. The armour of pride keeps us from learning.

Again, it keeps us from apprehending new truth, even in the deepest things. A great many minds are prejudiced against anything new and unfamiliar in religion, any new truth that sounds a little bit unorthodox or upsetting. And very often that is just the same armour of complacence and conceit—we won't believe we were wrong, we won't stretch our minds to consider anything new. In that way we often keep truth away from our minds, and it isn't good for us.

But above all, the armour of conceit keeps us from becoming better men and women. It keeps away the grace of God; grace and pride simply don't go together. The Bible tells us that 'God resisteth the proud, but giveth grace unto the humble'. Pride saves us no doubt from many humbling experiences, but thereby it keeps us from all moral and spiritual blessings.

In our Christian religion we talk a great deal about contrition and repentance and forgiveness and new beginnings; but very often we don't really give ourselves to these experiences. We are too proud. We don't want to be rebuked. We are not going to have ourselves continually upset. As we go about this world we would receive a good many hard knocks, and often find ourselves in the wrong, and frequently be made ashamed and have to acknowledge our shortcomings —if we were to allow ourselves to be touched and wounded in that way. But very often we won't. We are too proud. We encase ourselves in the armour of pride—we will see our neighbour's faults but not our own. That saves us the pains of penitence. But it is at a terrible cost. For it keeps us time after time from making a new start. It keeps us from turning our back on the past and becoming better men and women. It is not a good thing to keep ourselves safely encased in the armour of conceit.

(2) *The armour of the grace of God.* 'Not I,' said Paul, 'but the grace of God which was with me.' I believe that when Paul became a Christian he began to think far less about himself than he had been accustomed to do, and far more about God; far less about his own character and achievements, and far more about what God was giving him and doing for him. The result was that his own character began to grow far finer than ever and his achievements became far greater than ever. And he knew it. But he wasn't a bit conceited or complacent about it, because he would always say: 'Not I, but the grace of God which was with me.' And I am sure that is the secret of the Christian life and of that marvellous thing which we call the Christian character.

It has often been pointed out that the Christian character is full of the strangest contradictions; it is an extraordinary combination of apparently opposite qualities: strength and tenderness, the wisdom of the serpent and the harmlessness of the dove, pessimism and optimism, solemnity and joy; but above all, humility and confidence. What explains it? How can a man be both perfectly humble and perfectly confident? It is, of course, because he is always saying, consciously or unconsciously: 'Not I, but the grace of God.'

Here is a man faced with big responsibilities, a difficult enterprise, which seems beyond his powers of mind and will. He tackles it, without undue worry. He makes mistakes, perhaps big ones. But that doesn't make him give it up. Why not? Is it because he is conceited and won't see and admit his mistakes? Well, if that is the kind of man he is, the armour of conceit will indeed keep his pride from being wounded. But he won't be a success. He'll be a failure, because he will never learn from his mistakes. But if he is a real Christian, he will see his mistakes. He will admit them and regret them. But he won't give it all up because of them. He won't be wounded unto death. He has an armour to save him from that—not the armour of conceit, but the armour of God's grace.

All along he hasn't been thinking of himself, his own cleverness, his own prestige, but of God, who set him where he is and gave him his task to perform. And so he will try again, stronger and wiser than ever. And in the long run he will prove equal to his responsibilities, and yet won't be conceited about it, because it is 'Not I, but the grace of God'.

Again (and this is a still more vital and central case) here is a man who time after time, every week that he lives, every day that he lives, acknowledges and confesses his sins. Isn't it a wonder that he doesn't give up the business of Christian living altogether? He would, if he had nothing better for his defence than the armour of conceit. For the armour couldn't stand it, and a man would soon, with the bitterness of fallen pride, give it up as a bad job. What's the good of trying to go on, when every day, in spite of our repentances, we fall short again, and lose our tempers, or say something cruel or mean, or play the coward, or do some other little thing that makes us feel ashamed? What's the good of it?

If you want to know the Christian answer to that question, here it is: Don't think so much of yourself. Think of God. Don't think just of your own character stained again. Think of God—His will disobeyed, His love wounded, and nevertheless His grace still waiting for you, ready to accept you again. Think of Him.

That is the one thing that always makes it worth while to go on, to begin again, to rise up out of penitence into new hope, because God is willing to forgive you, and the great reality with which you have to do is not just yourself, your character, your merits—not you, but the grace of God.

Friends, I believe that is the very heart of the Gospel of Christ and the secret of living victoriously amid all the difficulties and vicissitudes of the world. The word 'grace' sounds mysterious (does it?)—just a bit of antiquated theological jargon. 'The grace of God'—what does that mean? And what has it got to do with the life of a practical hard-headed man or woman in this modern world?

I reply 'Everything'. I am sure that the really practical people, the really effective people, the really admirable and enviable people, are the people who have exchanged the armour of self-righteousness for the armour of the grace of God.

9. THE THREE CROSSES

And when they were come to the place which is called Calvary, there they crucified him, and the malefactors, one on the right hand, and the other on the left.
LUKE 23.33

THE subject before us here concerns the execution of a condemned man which took place by crucifixion, under the Roman Empire, in the Province of Judaea, more than nineteen centuries ago during the procuratorship of one Pontius Pilate. It was an event that set men thinking more than anything else that has ever happened in the history of the world. Countless books have been written about it, countless pictures of it have been painted, and the image of that figure on the Cross stands at the heart of our religion. It is indeed an extraordinary symbol to stand at the heart of any religion. Why should it be there?

In one of the Irish plays of William Butler Yeats there is a vivid scene which perfectly expresses the objection which the human heart so often and so naturally makes against the religion of the Cross. The scene is in a country cottage in Ireland. The family are sitting together in the firelight of the kitchen, and on the wall there hangs a black wooden crucifix. There is a knock at the door, and when it is opened, in comes a little fairy girl, dressed in green, singing a merry song, the very personification of natural pagan happiness and the spirit of the green woods. Suddenly her eyes fall upon the crucifix, and she stops her singing and hides her face, and cries out: 'Take down that ugly black thing.'

There is the revolt of the religion of nature—I might say of our human nature—against the religion of the Cross. How well it expresses the question that we have all sometimes wanted to ask: Why should Christianity take that gaunt and tragic emblem and set it up at the heart of its message and in the centre of its world? Why must Christianity make so much of the death of Jesus, of His Cross?

I want to suggest that one sound way of answering that question may be found—symbolically, but with a most natural and legitimate and even inevitable symbolism—in the words of our text. 'When they were come to the place which is called Calvary, there they crucified him, and the malefactors, one on the right hand and the other on the left.'

The Cross of Christ is not a solitary tragic cross, set up incongruously in the midst of a bright and happy world. It is a cross set between two other crosses, and we only understand its meaning when we look at the others too. Let us look then at the three crosses on Calvary.

(1) *The cross on the left hand* is tragic enough, sad and sordid enough. On it hangs a wretched criminal who is at odds with all the world, an outcast from society, and now dying an unspeakably painful and shameful death, with bitterness in his soul and at odds even with his fellow victims on that hill of Calvary.

That cross of the impenitent thief may well stand for all the sin and shame and suffering and tragedy of the world. That cross is the cross of all humanity. That man is everyman. And that cross explains why Jesus had to die, and why Christianity makes so much of His death.

We ask: Why does Christianity make so much of the Cross of Christ? In this fair and wonderful world, in which our hearts cry out for joy and feel that they were made for joy, why should the Christian religion introduce the Cross and make it dominate the landscape?

And the answer is: That is *not* what Christianity does or ever did. It was not Christianity that introduced the cross into the situation to cast its shadow. The cross was there already, and Christianity transfigured it. The cross was there already in ten thousand tragedies of human life. Quite literally, as I do not need to tell you, tens of thousands of men had died by crucifixion before Jesus did—tens of thousands of wretched thieves and murderers, rebels and runaway slaves. I wonder how many other crucifixions may have taken place in other spots all over the Roman Empire on that same spring morning on which Jesus was crucified. Even on that same spot, outside the gate of Jerusalem, there were two others.

Every schoolboy knew what it was to see the gaunt form of a cross standing out against the sky beside some highway, and to shudder as he passed. And that sums up all the sin and shame and pain of this fallen world. That was the situation into which Christianity came. That was the world with which it had to deal and which it had to save. And that is still the world we live in, as you very well know. You know very well too that it is not as though you and I could wash our hands of it. That impenitent thief—how much worse was he than the respectable people who passed comfortably by?

Perhaps he was more sinned against than sinning. Society could not wash its hands of him. He was the hapless victim, but the whole of society around was involved in the tangle of sin and shame that made an end of him. And we know that we are all involved in the tangle of sin and shame that has so many victims on the Calvaries of our time and has turned the world into a Golgotha.

Sometimes we are blind to it, sometimes we shut our eyes to it, and we want a romantic religion without a cross. But sometimes (and I am sure this happens to a great many young men and women in this present age), sometimes among all the sunshine and beauty we get a sudden vision of the immense tragedy of the life of humanity, and of our own share in the sinful responsibility for it, a sudden vision of the tens of thousands of shameful crosses that are destroying the life of mankind and the life of our souls.

And then we can thank God that Christianity has something to say about it. We can thank God that this Christian religion which has come down to us is a religion that faced the facts and went down into the depths and endured the Cross before it rose up to proclaim the victory and the glory of its Gospel. For the dreadful cross of humanity is always there—the cross of the impenitent thief.

(2) *The second cross, the one in the middle, is the cross of Christ.* It looks just the same as the others, and the passer-by would see no difference, except for the extraordinary superscription, which he could hardly take to be more than an ironical jest: Jesus of Nazareth, the King of the Jews! And yet Christian art has not gone astray when it has painted the central cross in such a perspective that it dwarfed the others and drew all eyes. For that Cross of Christ is indeed the central fact in the history of the world. It casts a new light on the other crosses. It has made the very word 'cross' into a new kind of word altogether.

In the ancient world it was a word of sordid shame, just like the word 'gallows' or 'gibbet' in the modern world. But it became a sacred word. St. Paul could speak of glorying in the Cross of Christ, and we can sing of 'the wondrous Cross on which the Prince of Glory died'. How did that Cross make such a difference? And what made it wondrous?

It was the One who hung on it and the spirit that was in Him as He embraced it.

We have grown so accustomed to the story of that divine drama of redemption in the subsequent light of the Christian faith that we commonly miss the element of terrible ordeal in the path that led our Lord to the Cross. We sometimes think of the crucifixion as if it were part of a prearranged drama in which our Lord had to play a settled part with a clear knowledge of the divine plot of the drama and of the triumphant conclusion. But it was much harder than that. He had to walk by faith and not by sight; and so far as sight could go, the cross that He saw looming doubtfully in His path must have looked as dreadful and final as anything could be, the very climax of shame and failure and tragedy, for Himself and for the people whom He had tried to serve and to save. The thing looked so dreadful that almost up to the last Jesus hoped and prayed that it might not come. If ever faith and love were difficult for any man in any situation, they were difficult for Jesus then. But Jesus went on with nothing in His heart except faith towards God and love towards men. And they crucified Him.

I said that the crucifixion of Jesus set men thinking more than anything else that has ever happened in the history of the world. And when men looked back and pondered on it, what did they think? This is the extraordinary thing: that it made them think of the love of God; not just of the love of Jesus, but of the love of God.

Of course they were looking back in the light of their resurrection faith. But they were looking back, surely, at the way in which Jesus had faced and endured the Cross. That was a new way of facing and overcoming evil. And it must be God's way. God must be like that. But was that precisely what they said, that God must be like Jesus? Nay, they said much more—God was in Jesus.

When Christ trod the *via dolorosa*, when Christ suffered and died, 'God was in Christ, reconciling the world unto himself'. God was not sitting remote in heaven, watching and judging the world from afar. God was there. God was involved in it, loving men with a love that would not give them up or let them go, however they might sin against it. This was God's own sacrifice. The victim was the Son of

God. This was God himself, bearing the brunt of the sin of men. This was the eternal love of God, bearing the sin and suffering of the world.

That is what men by stages learnt to say about the death of Jesus, and it is all over the New Testament. 'God commendeth his own love toward us, in that, while we were yet sinners, Christ died for us.' 'God so loved the world that he gave his only-begotten Son.' 'Herein is love, not that we loved God, but that he loved us, and sent his Son to be the propitiation of our sins.' And that was why St. Paul could say, 'God forbid that I should glory except in the cross of the Lord Jesus Christ.'

That is the cross that stands in the centre.

(3) *The third cross is the one on the right hand, the cross of the penitent thief.* You remember the story. The man acknowledges that he deserved crucifixion, and that Jesus did not. Then he cries to Jesus: 'Lord, remember me when thou comest into thy kingdom.' And Jesus replies: 'Verily I say unto thee, today shalt thou be with me in paradise.'

Now, I will not discuss, as an historical question, what exactly that conversation meant at the moment. That would take too long and would perhaps be too difficult. But there can be no doubt as to what it has come to signify in the whole context of the Christian message. It signifies something that the crucified Christ has done with the sin and suffering of men. It signifies the light which the Cross of Christ sheds on all the shameful crosses in the world—not the kind of light that explains, but the kind of light that redeems, calling men to repentance and forgiveness and a new beginning and a place in God's Kingdom of love and service. It signifies for all time what Christ has done with the sin and suffering of the world.

I spoke of how you and I sometimes have a sudden vision of that mass of sin and suffering, that perennial cross of humanity. When we have that sudden piercing vision, I believe our hearts sometimes tell us that we must give our lives to the noble crusade of liberating our fellows from evil and making the world a better place. But very soon our hearts fail us, because the evil is so immense; and we ask ourselves hopelessly whether our petty efforts can make any difference to the measureless mass of evil in this ruined world. Very soon also we ask ourselves what right we have to try to change the world for the better, we who are so deeply involved in its sin ourselves.

But what if God in Christ has borne and is bearing the mass of sin and suffering? What if God through the Cross of Christ is calling us to repentance, and offering to forgive us our sins? What if God is calling us, unworthy as we are, into His Kingdom, that we may be its children and its servants in the world, bearing our share of the cross of humanity in the power of the Cross of Christ?

Then everything becomes worth while again. Even our feeble endeavours to serve God among men become abundantly worth while: we know now that they will not be wasted, they cannot be lost, because they are caught up and purified and accepted and used in the invincible cause of God's everlasting Kingdom.

That is how Christ in His death, Christ reigning from the tree, stretches out His hands, to bless us with the forgiveness of our sins, and to call us into the service of His Kingdom. As St. Athanasius said sixteen hundred years ago, in words of magnificent symbolism: 'It is only on a cross that a man dies with outstretched hands.'

10. THE MYSTERY OF THE TRINITY

Without controversy great is the mystery of our religion. He was mani-fested in the flesh, vindicated in the spirit, seen by angels, preached among the nations, believed on in the world, received up into glory.
1 TIMOTHY 3.16

THIS morning I am going to make bold to preach about the doctrine of the Trinity. It comes constantly into our Christian worship—whenever we have the threefold Blessing at the close of a service, whenever we say or sing: 'Glory be to the Father and to the Son and to the Holy Ghost', or 'God in three Persons, Blessed Trinity.' What do we mean by it? Does it mean something that should make a difference to ordinary Christians in their daily Christian living? I would like to try to answer that question.

The text I have taken is not directly about the Holy Trinity, but it sums up in its own way what the doctrine of the Trinity stands for. It begins by asserting that our Chris-tian religion is a great mystery; and it goes on to bear that out by reciting the main facts of Christian belief in six short phrases. 'Without controversy great is the mystery of our religion. He was manifested in the flesh, vindicated in the spirit, seen by angels, preached among the nations, believed on in the world, received up into glory.'

That is a kind of compressed Creed, telling the story of the Incarnation, finishing with the Ascension, and with a phrase also about the work of the Holy Spirit. The Apostle appears actually to be quoting the words of a credal state-ment that was current in his time. But the words are more poetry than prose. The six short phrases seem to be balanced in an antiphonal arrangement with a rhythmical structure in the original Greek, as if for singing. And so scholars have conjectured that the Apostle is here quoting a stanza from an early Christian hymn. That gives the passage a peculiar interest. Here we have, apparently, a little bit of early Christian worship, a rhythmical stanza in which Christians were accustomed to sum up liturgically the main elements of Christian belief—those very facts about the Incarnation and the Holy Spirit that led to the formulation of the doctrine of the Trinity. And the Apostle quotes it to illustrate what he has just said about the great mystery of our religion.

So this text may serve to remind us of two great truths symbolized by the doctrine of the Trinity: how mysterious God is, and how accessible He is. Now let me say something about each of these in turn.

(1) *How mysterious God is!* 'Great is the mystery of our religion.' I am sure that is the first impression made on most people when the doctrine of the Trinity is mentioned; and often perhaps the only impression: that it is mystifying. 'Father, Son, and Holy Spirit, One God.' What does that mean? Whatever else it means, it makes you think at once how mysterious religion is, how mysterious God is. He is beyond your comprehension. You feel your mind reeling back helplessly from those dizzy heights. You are mystified.

Well, you ought to be. That is not at all an unwholesome effect. For there is a whole world of inscrutable mystery surrounding all our beliefs about God, and it is salutary to be made to realize it. Everything that we say or sing about God is but an attempt to put into our poor blundering human words something that can never be perfectly expressed in human words; stupendous divine realities too great to be grasped by human minds or comprehended in human categories. When we forget this, we are apt to become smug and self-satisfied, narrow-minded and intolerant, in our religious beliefs, as if we were in possession of the whole truth, and all other traditions must be wrong. We need to be reminded that God cannot be contained in any of our statements: He breaks through them all, and makes us think again.

> Our little systems have their day,
>   They have their day and cease to be.
>   They are but broken lights of Thee,
> And Thou, O Lord, art more than they.

All this is important even in connexion with our common worship, to keep it sound and Christian. Why do we observe all the solemn and stately forms of worship, with ritual and symbol and something of the language of poetry? Why do we perpetuate those strange services which we call sacraments: Baptism with water, in the name of the Father, the Son and the Holy Ghost; and the Sacrament of the bread and the wine? It is all very strange, and it may not seem to have anything to do with the simplicities of true religion. But it has. For our religion, with all its simplicity, is a great mystery. Not the kind of mystery that can be penetrated best by acute and learned minds, but the kind that is revealed to humble and childlike hearts. Yet it remains a great mystery, and these will be the first to acknowledge it.

Moreover, they will not be depressed or discouraged by it, but uplifted and exhilarated. Yes, it is good that God is so great, so high above our understanding. That is the kind of God we want and need, a God who escapes our words, and stretches our thoughts, so that we have to leave prose behind, and use all the symbol and sacrament and all the solemn and mysterious decorum of our Christian worship. The eighteenth-century German mystic Gerhard Tersteegen said: 'A God understood, a God comprehended, is no God.' And how often in the Bible that note is struck, the note of exhilaration at the thought of the mystery and majesty of God! St. Paul in one place breaks out with solemn thanks-

F

giving: 'O the depth of the riches both of the wisdom and knowledge of God. How unsearchable are his judgments, and his ways past finding out. . . . For who hath known the mind of the Lord? . . . For of him and through him and for him are all things: to whom be glory for ever.'

But mystery is not enough. It is a very good thing to have an aura of mystery round about every kernel of religious belief. But it would be a very poor thing to have the mystery without the kernel. We can't live on mere mystery. Moreover it is highly important to learn that in the New Testament this word 'mystery' never means sheer mystery. It always means a divine secret which it has pleased God to reveal to men; a secret so mysterious that we could never even begin to discover it for ourselves by a human search, if God had not taken the initiative and given us the clue. But He has done this in Jesus Christ and by His Holy Spirit. And so the mystery of our religion might be described as God's open secret: a floodlit patch of truth which fades off, all round about, into thick clouds and darkness, but which is enough to give us what we need, a faith to live by, in this rough-and-tumble world.

And that brings us to the second thing the doctrine of the Trinity has to say to us. It says not only: How mysterious God is, but also and chiefly:

(2) *How accessible God is!* How near, how approachable, how available, how inescapable, how present, how contemporary, every day, everywhere, with ordinary people in this ordinary world—the God who was once incarnate in Jesus, the God who gave His Holy Spirit at Pentecost, and who is as near now as He was then—'as it was in the beginning, is now, and ever shall be, world without end.'

The doctrine of the Trinity tells us all that. But it only tells us all that when it comes at the end of the Christian story. If it came at the beginning, it would be merely a mathematical puzzle about three-in-one and one-in-three. But it ought to come at the end, just as the season of Trinity comes at the end of the Christian year. And then it sums up the whole Christian story of what God has done for our salvation.

What a story it is, from start to finish! It begins with 'God manifest in the flesh', as our text puts it. That means the human life of Jesus of Nazareth, the Son of God Incarnate. To those disciples who rubbed shoulders with Him, who tramped the roads of Palestine with Him, that was by far the most marvellous experience they had ever known, and it brought God into their lives. That did not last long, for Jesus got into trouble with the authorities and was condemned to death and crucified. But that was only the beginning. Before long His disciples were convinced that even His shameful death had a plan of God in it for the salvation of men; and, moreover, He was not dead, but alive: He had risen from the dead and was at God's right hand.

But was He as far away as that? How could they get on without His presence in their midst on earth? How could they go on living without Him who had been the light of their lives? Did they collapse altogether when they were left to carry on? That was what we might have expected, and perhaps what they expected too. But that was not what happened. Something else happened, and those men realized that the wonderful Presence had come back to them in a new and more wonderful way. It came home to them suddenly on the date of a Jewish festival called Pentecost. The disciples and some others who had joined them were assembled in a room in Jerusalem for fellowship and prayer, when they suddenly had an overwhelming experience of the presence and power of God. Now they were quite sure that they had lost neither God nor Jesus. Now they could go anywhere and witness for Him. And they soon discovered that this great experience need not be confined to those who had known Jesus in the flesh. This was a thing that could come to anybody anywhere through the story of Jesus. It couldn't have come without Jesus, but it was something even greater and more universal than knowing Jesus in the flesh. It was something new in mankind's knowledge of God.

What was it? What were they to call it? Well, the disciples remembered something that an old prophet had predicted, and something that Jesus Himself had promised, about the gift of the Holy Spirit. And they said: Here it is. The thing has come true. This is the gift of the Holy Spirit of God poured out on men. God, our Heavenly Father, who was manifest in the flesh in His Son Jesus Christ, is with us now, and for ever more, through the Holy Spirit.

That is how Christians have come to speak of Father, Son, and Holy Spirit, One God. That is how the doctrine of the Trinity, coming at the end of the Christian story, is not a mere mystery, but sums up the whole Gospel, and speaks to us of how accessible God is, how near.

Do you see how it makes a difference? Perhaps you have sometimes tried to pray to God, and found your mind floundering in uncertain thought and imagination, not knowing how to conceive Him, feeling Him to be remote, unreal. And your heart has cried out under the brazen sky, with the ancient prophet: 'O that thou wouldst rend the heavens and come down.' But that is just what He has done in Jesus Christ: God manifest in the flesh. And so from all our floundering we come back to that—to the Gospel story, where we can hear Jesus speak, hear Him speak to God and hear Him speak to men. And we know at once that God is there. We can draw near to Him as He really is. Yet do we sometimes wish we could have lived in the time of Christ, or that He could have lived in our time, so that we need not strain our eyes to look into a distant past, but have Him beside us now? But we do have Him, even closer than many who rubbed shoulders with Him in Galilee. Through the Gospel of Christ we have that even greater and more wonderful presence which God gives us through the Holy Spirit.

So this is the truth of the doctrine of the Trinity. The God who was incarnate in Jesus is not far away in high heaven. Nor is He far back through time in ancient Palestine. He is near. He is here. He has done all that could be done to make Himself accessible. He besets us behind and before: we cannot go from His Spirit, or escape from His presence. At this very hour He is pressing in upon everyone of us with His inexorable love; to awaken us, to challenge us, to judge us, to claim us, to befriend us, to redeem us. Father, Son and Holy Spirit. Therefore, with fear and trembling, with faith and love, with gratitude and adoration, we can join the whole Church of God and say: 'Glory be. . . .'

11. WATCH AND PRAY

Watch and pray, that ye enter not into temptation. St. Mark 14.38

Jesus addressed these words to three of His disciples, Peter,
James and John, in a group by themselves in the Garden of
Gethsemane. How then did St. Mark, who wrote this story
in his Gospel, come to know about them? How could he
report what was said? The answer is that he heard about it
afterwards from Simon Peter. That is not mere guesswork,
for there is an ancient Church tradition which tells us that
Mark knew Peter intimately and that his Gospel is based on
Peter's reminiscences of the life of our Lord. Now when we
read St. Mark's Gospel in the light of that information, many
points stand out with a new interest. For there is a great deal
in it about Peter, and sometimes it is not to his credit—it
tells of foolish things he said and did, rebukes that he received
from his Master, and so on. And when we read about them
and remember that all this comes from Peter's own reminiscences, we feel as if we were listening to Peter as a humble
Christian man in after days looking back and making his
confessions, for the benefit of other people.

Now just apply that to the passage of our text. Jesus is
with His disciples in the Garden of Gethsemane on the very
night before His crucifixion. He knows what lies ahead, and
how severely He and His disciples are going to be tested and
tried within the next twelve hours. It will put a tremendous
strain on their courage and devotion, and they ought to be
preparing for it in the presence of God. Jesus Himself spent
the time in prayer to His Father. And He strongly urged
Peter and James and John to do the same. It was one of the
great nights in the history of the world, and He knew well

that amid the dreadful things that were going to happen His
disciples would be exposed to the most serious temptation
of their lives, the temptation to lose courage and desert their
Master in His hour of danger. So He said to them, time after
time: 'Watch and pray, that ye enter not into temptation.'

We know what happened. The disciples did not take His
advice. They did not take it seriously. They were tired, they
were sleepy, they were not inclined for prayer (perhaps they
had not had much practice in it), and they kept falling asleep.
And then the danger came, the terrible reality, a party of
armed men in the semi-darkness, a band of police and soldiers
and rabble to arrest Jesus and carry Him off to prison. We
know how Jesus behaved. He was prepared in spirit. He
had been communing with God in prayer; now He was calm
and strong, resting on the will of God, steady and ready for
everything, and He faced the danger and cruelty, and went
through the dreadful events of that night and next morning
with faith and hope and love as God's own Son. But the
disciples were not ready, and they lost their heads and their
courage. They went through that great night of nights in the
history of the world, and never rose to the occasion, but
gave way to the temptation. They all deserted their Master
and ran away. And an hour or two later Simon Peter, who
thought he was the most loyal of them all, lost his courage
again and denied his Master three times, in the early morning
of the great tragic day on which his Master was crucified.
He used to tell it himself, long afterwards, and he told Mark,
who wrote it down in his Gospel.

What did Simon Peter feel like when he came to himself
and realized what he had done? He told that also, and it is
enough to set our imaginations working. He wept. He had
done something which he could not have believed possible.
He, Simon Peter, whom his Master had called the Rock,
who had been so keen, so loyal, who had made such pro-

testations of courage and faithfulness, now he had played the coward, he had failed his Master in His hour of need, he had repudiated his Master at the supreme moment, he had been overcome by the temptation to play for safety and to let his Master stand alone, How and why had he done it? How had it come about? How had he come to such a pass? It was because he had not been spiritually ready. He had allowed himself to face the events of that night in a worldly and trivial and selfish frame of mind. He had not taken the trouble to prepare himself spiritually in the presence of God. And he only realized it when it was too late. Mark tells us that when Peter heard the cock crowing, he remembered how his Master had told him: 'Before cockcrow this very night, you will deny me.' But he also remembered another thing his Master had said. He remembered how, among the trees, in the half-light of the Garden, only a few hours before, Jesus had said: 'Watch and pray, lest you enter into temptation.' If only he had taken Jesus' advice! Then he would have been ready, and would have played the man. He would have faced the temptations of that night with clear vision and calm will and strong faith, because he had been placing his soul in the presence of God, because he had watched and prayed. But—he hadn't watched and prayed. He hadn't taken his Master's advice. So he wasn't prepared. And now it had come to this, he had denied his Master, and only wakened up from his spiritual slumber when it was too late and the thing was done. He confessed it all afterwards, and there it stands for us in the Gospel story.

Now the reason why all that is so deeply interesting to us is that it is so extraordinarily like what sometimes happens to ourselves, in small matters if not in large. Have you never had the experience of being overtaken unawares by some temptation and yielding to it almost before you were aware that it was a temptation? Have you never in that sense been caught napping, and then wakened up spiritually to discover that you had done something to be ashamed of? I do not mean great betrayals, flagrantly disgraceful things, but the little betrayals that come so easily, but which you never really intended or expected to commit, because they are quite unworthy of your Christian profession and you had often made resolutions against them. It may be a case of moral cowardice—a little like Peter's, only with far less excuse. One day perhaps in some company where you find yourself things are being said that you ought as a Christian to speak up against, but you haven't the courage to show your true colours, and you say nothing, you just acquiesce in what is being said, and in that negative way at least you deny your Master; and when it is all over you see what you have done. Or it may be that in talking to somebody you receive sudden provocation, something touches your pride, and you suddenly lose your temper, and you say something bitter and foolish and unjust, something unworthy of a Christian. Or you find yourself in a tight corner, with a choice to make between saving your own skin, serving your own interests, and doing the generous thing out of consideration for other people; and before you know where you are, you find your-self making the selfish choice and letting other people down. Or in some other way you are overtaken by a subtle tempta-tion, 'the lust of the flesh, the lust of the eyes, or the pride of life'. And a moment later you realize that you have yielded to it; and you ask yourself how you came to do such a thing when you had often made resolutions against it. Like Peter, you wake up and see what you have done; and you wonder why.

And what is the answer? The answer is (just as with Peter) that you lost the battle because you weren't ready. And you weren't ready, most probably, because you had been slack about the life of prayer, you had begun the day, and perhaps many days, without really seeking the presence of God, that you might walk all day in the light of His countenance. And the lesson of all that, as Peter knew so well, is just what you find in the words of our text: 'Watch and pray, that ye enter not into temptation.'

Therefore let me now, in the light of that story, say a few words to you about the place that *Prayer* ought to have in the life of a Christian man or woman. A great many people think of prayer as merely an occasional thing, an application made to God now and then for something we want. But we ought to think of prayer as a constant regular thing without which we cannot truly live, a daily exercise in the presence of God without which our souls cannot be healthy and therefore cannot throw off the germs of temptation. It isn't enough to wait till the temptation is upon us and then send up a cry to God for help. Often there is no time for that— it may be too late, temptation comes so suddenly and takes us by surprise. The holy war we have to fight is a mobile war, highly 'motorized' (as we would say), with rapid spear-heads, with lightning strokes, with a constant, element of tactical surprise, with racing columns of the enemy darting in and out, here and there, appearing behind us as well as in front of us. That is what temptation is like in this world. And unless we are always ready, we shall be taken unawares, like the German general during the war in France who was taken prisoner while he was at his breakfast.

Do you remember how St. Paul expresses it? 'Put on the whole armour of God, that ye may be able to stand against the wiles of the Devil. For our wrestling is not against flesh and blood, but against principalities and powers, against the world-rulers of this darkness, against the spiritual hosts of wickedness.' He means, of course, the war against temptation and sin. 'Wherefore,' he says, 'take up the whole armour of God, that ye may be able to stand in the evil day, and having done all, to stand.' And then he goes on to speak of what the armour is: 'the girdle of truth, the breastplate of righteousness, the shoes of peace, the shield of faith, the helmet of salvation, and the sword of the Spirit, which is the word of God.' Plainly he does not mean that we should snatch up the armour and put it on when we see the enemy approaching. If you wait for that in this mobile warfare it is too late. He means and he says that we should stand in that armour constantly, so that we can never be taken by surprise.

And what does that mean in actual practice? How does one get and put on that spiritual armour? St. Paul leaves no doubt about it. In the very next verse he goes on to say (almost as if he were thinking of our Lord's words in the Garden) that the way to do it is to watch and pray, and to do it constantly and regularly, not only for ourselves but for one another. And that means the whole regular practice of Bible reading, and meditation in God's presence, and communion with Him, and petition and intercession directed to Him through Jesus Christ our Lord, in public worship, of course, and in family worship, but also very specially (because this needs to be said) in our own private times of devotion each day. How difficult it is to find time—even a little time —for such devotion in this busy world! But wouldn't it be worth the trouble if it really sent us forth into the world each day clad with the armour of God?

If we could learn something of that practice, if we could every day breathe in something of that fresh air of God, and take that wholesome exercise for our souls, then we would go out into the world in such good spiritual health that our souls would throw off the infection of evil as a healthy body throws off the germs of disease. And we should not so often have to deplore that we had betrayed or denied our Master.

12. THE STATUTES TURNED INTO SONGS

Thy statutes have been my songs in the house of my pilgrimage.
PSALM 119.54

THAT great Scottish patriot Fletcher of Saltoun said: 'Let me make the songs of a country, and let who will make its laws.' But this ancient Hebrew Psalmist says something better still. He says that for him the laws have become songs, to inspire him on his way through life. As Dr Moffatt translates it: 'Thy statutes are my songs, as I wander through the world.' In fact, though the Psalmist lived long before the dawn of the gospel of Christ, he had travelled a long way towards it —you might say he had already got half-way between the law and the gospel. To him the good life was no longer a mere commandment, to be kept with a weary and grudging effort. No, he had entered so much into the spirit of it that it was more like a bit of music.

In his charming book *In Search of England* H. V. Morton tells us of an experience he had in Winchester Cathedral. He was up in the tower, among the bells, with a party of visitors under the guidance of the verger—a mixed crowd, he says. The verger numbered them all, gave each of them a bell-rope, and then pointed to each in turn as he wished them to ring their bell; and so he drew forth from that unpromising assembly the tune of 'Abide with me'. Morton says: 'We were delighted with ourselves.' But of course it wasn't music. They all did what they were told, but you can't get music by commandment.

By way of contrast, think of a group of men and women united in a good orchestra, engaged in a Beethoven symphony. Again each individual has his own instrument, and

82

again they all take their directions from one man who is conductor. But what a contrast between the two ideas, and between the two results! In the orchestra there is nothing mechanical. Everyone has a grasp of the music, everyone is loyal to the conductor, everyone has entered into the spirit of the symphony, and takes delight in contributing his part, with understanding and with enthusiasm. The symphony carries them on, lifts them all above themselves into a kind of supernatural achievement. That is music. That is the real thing.

What a good parable of the real Christian life! The real Christian life is not mere morality, a matter of always 'toeing the line', and then being 'delighted with yourself', like those stodgy people in the tower of Winchester Cathedral who pulled a bell-rope when they were told. There wasn't a breath of the spirit of music there. And the Christian life ought to make music. 'Thy statutes have been my songs in the house of my pilgrimage.'

What a difference it makes when we have that really Christian attitude! We shall take two different departments of conduct as illustrations.

(1) Take that problem of *Sunday observance*. On this question one often finds people divided sharply into two opposite camps—the strict Sabbatarians on the one side and the Libertarians on the other. And very often both parties are on a false trail, and fundamentally they are making the same mistake—both are looking at it in a too legal spirit, as if it were a matter of law, while it is really a matter of gospel. They have not learned to turn the statute into a song.

Strict Sabbatarians sometimes speak as if we had nothing to do but quote an ancient Hebrew law from the Old Testament, 'Remember the sabbath day to keep it holy,' and they take it simply to mean that on a certain day every week you must never do anything you can avoid doing. What a poor

negative uninspired way of looking at it! Jesus had no use
for that kind of thing—it is quite plain from the gospel story.
He said 'The sabbath was made for man, and not man for
the sabbath,' and that meant a quite different way of looking
at it. And as for His disciples, when a little later they began
to keep the Lord's Day (which is what we now keep, as
Christians), well, that wasn't the Sabbath at all, but something much better. It wasn't the last day of the week, but
the first; and it was a day on which you do certain things—
splendid, joyful things, acts of worship and fellowship, lifting
you above the work-a-day world, because it is the Lord's
Day, the day when Christians remember the victory of Jesus
Christ. There is no definite Christian law as to what you
may do and what you must not do on Sunday—it is something
far better than a law. Sabbatarians need to remember that.

But then the Libertarians need it just as much. For they
are apt to make just the same mistake. They treat it as a
matter of law. They say: 'Prove to me that it is wrong to do
such and such a thing on Sunday, and if you can't, then I'll
begin doing it.' They ask: 'Is there any harm in playing
games on Sunday?' As if that were ever a healthy kind of
criterion for a Christian. The Christian is pledged to aim at
the very highest and to make the very best of every gift.
Therefore the question for a virile Christian is: What is the
very best kind of use that we as individuals and as a community or as a nation can make of this one day in seven which
by long tradition has been kept free from the ordinary work
of the world? If we could all come to look at the question
as eager, responsible Christians, one result would be that we
would be far less ready to criticize others for things they do
on Sunday; and another would be that we would make a far
better use of Sunday ourselves. 'Thy statutes have become
my songs'—that's what is wanted.

(2) Again, let us apply the same principle to the question

of *moral purity*. Here, again, people often think of it as if it were merely a mysterious law, arbitrarily laid down by God, that we mustn't do certain things. People say, as it were: 'These animal instincts that I feel in me are somehow wrong and wicked because God has chosen to call them wicked; but I don't know why. And if they are wicked, I don't know why they are in human nature at all. But I suppose I must just toe the line, and suppress them and live a pure life.' But what a sad, weary way to look at the matter—as if God had given us nothing more than the Seventh Commandment. When people take it in that way, they don't usually make a very good job of it. They don't attain a very inward kind of purity, and if they do manage half against their wills to maintain an outward standard of purity, in a grudging spirit, they usually become very uncharitable towards those who have fallen.

If we're going to be Christians we must learn a far better secret of purity than that. For one thing, we must learn that those instincts and appetites are not wrong in themselves. But, for another thing, we must learn that they can make awful havoc of human life unless we use them as God meant us to use them. But there is a third thing we have to learn: that the laws of purity can't be kept by a mere dull negative effort, in the spirit of a galley-slave under a slave-driver. To quote a famous saying (from Sir John Seeley): 'No heart is pure that is not passionate; no virtue is safe that is not enthusiastic.' The only way to save the soul from lust is to get the heart filled with love—the love of God and man, the noble enthusiasm of the Christian life. That is something big enough to catch up and use and ennoble and glorify every instinct and appetite, and that is what is really meant by Christian purity.

Don't try to make the Christian life a poor, dull, negative business. It is a matter of hearing the voice of Jesus, and, like the disciples by the Lake of Galilee, rising up wholeheartedly to follow Him, with a new enthusiasm and a new treasure which can make music in our hearts, and make our lives to run on like music; so that we are lifted above our temptations, and His statutes become our songs.

But there is one thing more to be said. That happy result does not happen completely all at once. It does not happen completely in this earthly life at all. Because, after all, this earthly life is 'the house of our pilgrimage' and not our ultimate home. Sometimes we don't want to do God's will. It is bound to be so during the period of our pilgrimage. That is why the statute is needed like a hedge to fence in our path. But the longer we go on in the path of our pilgrimage, the more does the statute turn into a song, and we march on to its music—we 'run in the way of his commandments', because God with His love has 'enlarged our hearts'.

13. THE PEACE OF GODLESSNESS
OR THE PEACE OF GOD

And he was in the hinder part of the ship, asleep on a pillow.
MARK 4.38

THERE are two places in Scripture where we have a picture of a man lying fast asleep in a boat in the middle of a raging storm.

The first place is in the story of Jonah. You remember that ship which he took at the port of Joppa, bound for Tarshish, that he might escape from Jehovah and his unpleasant duty; and how a terrible storm came upon the ship, and the crew were in great trepidation. 'But,' says the storyteller, 'Jonah was gone down into the inner parts of the ship; and he lay, and was fast asleep.' That was a scene on a big vessel on the Mediterranean Sea.

And then here in the Gospels we have a similar touch in a story of a storm on the Lake of Galilee. It was a little fishingboat, manned by disciples of Jesus who until recently had been fishermen themselves. And a sudden storm sprang up, one of those squalls which would be very common on that little inland sea surrounded by hills. The fishermen were in a great panic. 'But,' says Mark, 'Jesus was in the stern, asleep on the cushion.'

The comparison of these two pictures, and the contrast between them, may give us something to reflect upon. We may use them as parables of human life, as illustrating two very different kinds of mental tranquillity and peace.

It might perhaps seem fanciful to put together two such different stories, from such different parts of the Bible. Only it seems quite likely, as some scholars have thought, that St.

87

Mark himself was conscious of the similarity when he wrote his story. Of course he knew the story of Jonah well, and from the way in which he tells this story of Jesus, from the language he uses, and especially from the turn of expression in this verse of our text, it seems that perhaps he had the older story of Jonah in mind. And if *he* was thinking of the one while he was writing the other, we may well put the two side by side.

Moreover, a great number of readers have been struck by the similarity. In each of the stories you have the man sleeping peacefully through the storm. And in each you have the crew coming to waken him, and they ask the sleeper wonderingly how he can lie there through the danger.

These are the resemblances. But then, with all that outward resemblance, there is an inward difference between these two sleepers. Jonah was at ease because he thought he had escaped from God; while Jesus was at peace because He was sure of God's love and care. And it just reminds us that there are these two kinds of tranquillity—the tranquillity of unbelief and the tranquillity of faith; the peace of godlessness and the peace of God.

Let us think of these two kinds.

(1) *The peace of godlessness.* This voyage of Jonah's was a godless voyage. He had shaken off responsibility, put God and duty and heroism and idealism out of his life for the time. Having left the land of Israel behind, he thinks he has left its God behind too, and his mind is easy now, he doesn't care. So he sleeps soundly.

Of course it is true that when God does come into our lives He does trouble us. And so some people succeed in preserving their tranquillity by leaving out all the pains of aspiration, all the struggles and strivings after better things, all the hard plodding of the path of duty, all the pains of sympathy and pity, all the burden-bearing which this sad

88

world needs. They go on their way sleek and comfortable, with never a sleepless hour of the night for their own sins or their brother's needs. They are quite contented and happy and peaceful in the midst of this great spiritual drama of human life, though there is nothing in their hearts and lives but the world and self and getting and spending and comfort and pleasure. And there is nothing noble or beautiful or enviable about that kind of tranquillity.

Some people succeed in preserving that mean kind of tranquillity in their hearts all their lives long. But I must go on to say that we are nearly all tempted to seek that kind of tranquillity. It is so easy in this world to become engrossed in getting and spending and enjoying oneself, and so to go through life easy and happy in a shallow kind of way. We are all apt to run away like Jonah from duty and responsibility and God, and so to find a worldly tranquillity, like Jonah asleep in the cabin of the ship.

But if there is anything divine in us at all (and there is some spark of the Divine in every one of us), then we can never find a very deep peace in that way. And I dare say most of the people who seem to be absolutely contented with the world know in their own hearts that they have not found the secret of happiness and peace. Theirs is not a very deep peace, the peace of the world.

(2) *The tranquillity of faith, the peace of God.* I don't think it is fanciful to find a parable of that in the picture of Jesus asleep. I think that is the great interest and charm of this story of the storm on the lake—that it shows us the bearing and behaviour of Jesus in a situation of real physical danger. Jesus was absolutely cool and collected and calm, and He was surprised at the panic of the disciples, surprised that men who professed to be religious should lose all the calm of their religion in a moment of danger. 'Why are you afraid?', He asked. 'Haven't you got faith yet?' *He* had. He really

believed in God, believed that they were all in God's keeping. So He had the calm and courage of faith.

And so it was throughout the life of Jesus. He bore the burdens of all men and the burdens of the Kingdom of God, but He bore them without worry, He carried about with Him the peace of God.

Yes, and He was always recommending that way of facing life to the common people around Him. They had their own worries, those common cares which are the same in all lands and in all centuries. You might think that with the worry of it all they would have no leisure of mind to listen to a preacher of religion like Jesus. Ah, but the religion He brought was just for such people in such a workaday world as ours; and Jesus Himself knew all about it, for He Himself had come from a humble home. And His message to these people was not to worry, and His cure for worry was to trust in God. He said: 'O you people of little faith. Do not worry with "What shall we eat?" and "What shall we drink?" and "Wherewithal shall we be clothed?" These are the things the Gentiles seek, but your heavenly Father knows you need all these things. *You* seek His Kingdom, and all these things shall be added unto you.' He actually told these poor people, with all their cares, not to worry, to stop worrying about their livelihood, and bravely trust in God; and then they would have peace and leisure of mind to turn to the quest of God's Kingdom. And then, in the spiritual cares of God's Kingdom too, He would not have people worry. There also they were to trust in God's love and power. 'Fear not, little flock; it is your Father's good pleasure to give you the Kingdom.'

Apparently that was one of the characteristic things in the original Christianity: that secret of getting away from worry to the peace of God. We find it repeatedly in the New Testament. Thus we read: 'When you are brought before judges for my sake, do not worry beforehand as to what you are to say; for it will be given you in that hour what you are to say.' And again Paul, who had learned his Master's secrets so well, says to his friends at Philippi: 'Do not worry about anything, but make your wants known to God by prayer and supplication, with thanksgiving. And the peace of God, which passes all understanding, will keep your hearts and minds in Christ Jesus.' That was an alternative to worry, a better way than the way of anxiety—this method of committing one's way to God and bringing one's wants to Him. And the result, Paul said, would be a wonderful inexplicable kind of peace, a peace which couldn't be accounted for by anything in the outward circumstance, a peace which went beyond one's understanding; for it depended, not on the absence of trouble, but on this habit of keeping the soul with all its wants turned to God.

In our day, as in Christ's day and in Paul's, most lives have plenty of troubles and cares. And there is nothing on earth more difficult than to keep from worrying about them, to rise above anxiety into peace. But let us realize that our Christianity ought to teach us in some degree to do it. We ought to know something, amid all our cares, of what it is to trust in God and so to be kept in peace. It should not be always just anxious days and restless nights. 'It is vain for you to rise up early, and lie down late, and eat the bread of sorrows, for God giveth his beloved sleep'—sleep like Jesus, in the midst of the storm.

14. NEW YEAR

Let not the wise man glory in his wisdom, neither let the mighty man glory in his might, let not the rich man glory in his riches: But let him that glorieth glory in this, that he understandeth and knoweth me, that I am the Lord which exercise lovingkindness, judgment, and righteousness, in the earth: for in these things I delight, saith the Lord.

JEREMIAH 9.23, 24

IN that remarkable book *Revolt in the Desert* by T. E. Lawrence there is a passage which may be taken as a kind of introduction to this text.

One night in the summer of 1917, while the First Great War was raging, Colonel Lawrence was out in the Arabian desert with his mixed force of Arabs. He and a few of the chiefs were sitting on their carpets around a camp fire under the stars. One of the Arabs began lazily to look at the stars through Lawrence's field-glasses. 'And the stars—what are they?' someone asked. That set them talking of the suns beyond suns and of how, when telescopes were still further improved, thousands upon thousands of new stars would be discovered; until, as one of the Arabs then said, 'When we see them all, there will be no night in heaven.' Then another of the Arabs broke in impatiently: 'Why are the Westerners always wanting everything? Behind our few stars we can see God, and He is not to be found beyond your millions.' Then the questioning imaginative one began again: 'Are there men on these greater worlds? And has each one got the Prophet, and Heaven, and Hell?' But the impatient one broke in again: 'Lads, we know our districts and our camels and our women. . . . The rest is God's and the glory is God's. If the end of wisdom is to add star to star, our foolishness is better.' And he immediately turned the conversation to the subject of money, until all the tongues began to buzz at once.

In that quiet hour under the stars, on the sand of the Arabian desert, those men were thinking thoughts that did not often come to them. They saw themselves and all their world so little in the midst of the great universe, and they began to ask themselves unusual questions about God and the universe and what things are really worth while for man in this world.

That is precisely what we think about sometimes as we watch the passing of an old year and the coming of a new. At twelve o'clock last night this earth of ours, sailing through space, completed another of its long journeys round the sun, as we measure them on our calendar. We little creatures living on its surface have completed another year of our short existence on this earth. Perhaps some of you woke up this New Year's morning asking questions, in the light of these immensities and eternities, as to what the meaning of life really is and what things are really worth while for us men and women upon earth.

And the answer, for us, and for those Arabs of the desert, comes in the words of our text, in the words of an old Oriental prophet, who spoke in a language much more like theirs than like ours.

Think of each of the clauses of the text in turn, taking that desert scene as a background.

(1) *Let not the wise man glory in his wisdom.* The wisest men never do it. But there is a sense in which we are very apt to do it in the modern world. The progress of scientific knowledge has been a very wonderful thing in modern times. But the old Arab asked: 'What will happen with this increasing knowledge?' 'When we see all the stars, there will be no night in heaven'—and he meant that there would be no room left for mystery, for God. If that was to be the

ultimate end of all our Western wisdom, they didn't want it. Well, these were foolish Arabs with timid lazy oriental minds. We don't want that; we want knowledge, we want truth.

But wasn't there some truth in what they said? Quite a number of Eastern countries are being flooded with European scientific teaching which is breaking up their old religions and putting nothing positive in their place. And the result is disastrous—either sheer materialism, or, worse still, a new and more dangerous paganism. But the same danger exists even in Christian countries like our own. In this twentieth century we need very badly to learn over again the lesson that progress in every other kind of knowledge is a poor thing unless it goes with the knowledge of God. It would be good for us to pray the beautiful prayer written by Francis Bacon, the founder of modern science and philosophy: 'We humbly and earnestly ask that human things may not prejudice such as are divine, so that from the opening of the gates of sense and the kindling of a greater natural light, nothing of incredulity or intellectual might may arise in our minds towards divine mysteries; but rather, O Lord, that our minds being thoroughly cleansed and purged from fancy, and yet subject to the divine will, there may be given unto faith the things that are faith's, that so we may continually attain to a deeper knowledge and love of Thee.'

(2) *Let not the mighty man glory in his might.* There are two thoughts that sometimes chasten and subdue men when they are tempted to glory in their might. The one is the kind of thought that came to men in the desert under the stars—the sense of the immensity of this material universe, dwarfing man into insignificance. 'When I consider the heavens— the moon and the stars—what is man?' And the other kindred thought is the one that comes to us at the passing of the old year—the sense of the length of eternity and the brevity of human life.

When we are young we feel as if we had endless time stretching out in front of us on earth. When we are in the full flush of our powers and activities we have a sense of mastery and self-sufficiency in the universe, and we sometimes try to do without God. We are ready to glory in our might. But at the passing of an old year, we realise vividly that our time is passing.

Now that does not mean tragedy and defeat for those who really believe in the gospel. It is not sad for Christian men and women; because God has given us eternal life; and we can think quite calmly and gladly of the brevity of life. But without that—without God, without Christ, without the meaning He gives to life, without anything to glory in but our own might, and our selfish use of it—New Year's Day must be one of the saddest days in all the year.

(3) *Let not the rich man glory in his riches.* That is the commonest danger of all, and not only for the rich man, but for the ordinary man.

Those Arabs were speaking of the stars and God and His glory, but very soon the conversation turned round to money, and presently the Arab who had been talking of giving the glory to God began whispering to Colonel Lawrence about the reward he hoped to get from King Feisal when the campaign was over. That was rather an anti-climax. But it is so true to life. It so often comes back to that in the end—material gain and prosperity. That is the great snare: to become wholly absorbed in the business of making a good living, without even stopping to ask yourself what you are living for. Jeremiah saw people doing that when he wrote this text. Jesus saw people doing it, and He spoke sadly of how people got obsessed with 'the cares of this world and the deceitfulness of riches', so that they had no time to think of God's Kingdom.

But that kind of life is so poor I hardly need stop to point

95

out its poverty. If you've got nothing more than that out of the year, you have got nothing out of it at all.

(4) We come at last to the one thing worth while. *But he that glorieth, let him glory in this, that he understandeth and knoweth me, that I am the Lord, which exercise lovingkindness, judgment and righteousness in the earth: for in these things do I delight, saith the Lord.* Jeremiah wrote these words between two and three thousand years ago in Palestine, and they still stand in all their simplicity and profundity; and we cannot go beyond them—except that we can put a yet deeper and brighter meaning into them through the gospel of Jesus; as Paul did when he said: 'God forbid that I should glory save in the cross of the Lord Jesus Christ.'

As an old year passes and a new year comes, don't these things stand out as the things that matter: to know God, to have Him as our Father and our Friend, to get His loving-kindness and righteousness into our hearts, so that it overflows into our lives? What else matters? And above all in this unstable terrifying modern world, what else matters?

We can begin the year with gladness and look forward into it with hope, if we have—God, the God and Father of our Lord Jesus Christ. God is working His purpose out. God's counsel standeth for ever. God's Kingdom cannot fail. And God calls us into the fellowship and service of His Kingdom, that in this bewildering modern world we may live as His sons and daughters, working with Him for the good of mankind, with His love in our hearts.

That gives life a meaning. That makes life worth living. Therefore I wish you all a good New Year.

15. THE FULNESS OF THE GOSPEL

The fulness of the blessing of the gospel of Christ.
ROMANS 15.29

ACCORDING to the Revised Version, it reads 'the fulness of the blessing of Christ', leaving out the word gospel, and no doubt that is what St. Paul wrote, though we are rather sorry to have the familiar verse changed. But it doesn't make any difference to the meaning. My subject is the importance of a complete Christianity—not a one-sided version of it, but the whole of it.

The reason I take this subject is because people are so apt to leave out one or another of the essential elements of the gospel; and so my best plan will be to indicate these different kinds of one-sidedness.

(1) *Don't forget His teaching.* That is what evangelical Christians sometimes almost leave out—the plain practical ethical teaching of Jesus, the Sermon on the Mount, the Golden Rule and all it carries with it.

What a large part of His time Jesus spent in teaching, and how much of His teaching is practical moral teaching as to how we ought to live! There is no doubt Jesus Himself attached a tremendous amount of importance to that part of the gospel—the doing of God's will in actual daily practice. 'Why call ye me Lord, Lord, and do not the things which I say?' 'Not every one that saith unto me, Lord, Lord, shall enter into the kingdom of heaven; but he that doeth the will of my Father.' What could be plainer than that? And there is the solemn parable that stands at the close of the Sermon on the Mount, telling us that the man who hears Christ's words and doesn't do them is like a man who built his house on sand, while the man who hears and does them is like a man who has built his house on a rock.

Yet evangelical Christians sometimes aren't very fond of the Sermon on the Mount—as if it weren't part of the real gospel. Remember that it is in the Sermon on the Mount, in the very forefront of that mighty challenge, that we find the Beatitudes, which tell us of the secret of the blessing. 'Blessed are the meek, blessed are the merciful,' and so on. Fogazzaro has spoken somewhere with satire of 'the people who believe in the miracles, but don't believe in the Beatitudes'. Such people are not uncommon. And yet if you don't take the Beatitudes seriously, you are far away from the blessing of Christ.

But let us not speak of other people. Let us think of ourselves. Some of you must have read that remarkable book, *The Life of Kagawa*, the Japanese saint, surely one of the greatest Christians living in the world today. There is a man who *lives* Christianity, spending his own money recklessly on schemes for rescuing the down and out, living in poverty, a friend of sinners, overcoming evil with good, claiming nothing for himself; and yet finding the radiant joy of Christianity, the beatitude of the gospel, because he does take the Sermon on the Mount seriously. It makes us wonder why we aren't trying to do it more. We know that we could, every day, find occasions of being more just and considerate to our neighbours, more merciful to our enemies, more unselfish, more willing to lose our lives, for Christ's sake, in love for other people. If you want the blessing of His gospel, don't forget His teaching.

(2) *Don't leave out His Cross.* That is another mistake that other people make, sometimes the very people who are keen on His teaching.

When we do first get captivated by the wonder and truth

of the teaching of Jesus we are apt to say that is all that is needed, that is Christianity—that, and not any mysteries of atonement and salvation. It is a noble, a divine way of living. If only everybody would live like that, then the world would become like heaven on earth.

Yes, if . . . ! And that is just where we discover that we need a completer gospel than that. I believe that in the modern world, up to the War and even beyond it, there has been a good deal of the rather easy optimism which believed that good teaching alone could put the world right—a mild and benevolent and hopeful humanitarianism. But people are discovering that the world is far more difficult to redeem than they imagined. I wonder whether we mightn't say reverently that even Jesus Christ had to make that discovery as His ministry went on. He found that human nature, with all its possibilities of good, has also all sorts of kinks and twists, and it doesn't always respond at once to good teaching like the Golden Rule. And so the career of Jesus Christ went on from the Sermon on the Mount to the Cross on the Hill. He practised the Golden Rule, but they responded by shedding His blood.

Well, that Cross, ever since, has been part of the gospel, indeed the very heart of it. It speaks to us not only of the evil that is in human nature, but also of the power that is in divine love. It speaks to us not only of the love of Jesus, but thereby also of the love of God, which bears the sin of the world. It speaks to us of how sin can be forgiven, and good brought out of evil, because God loves us. And 'God commendeth his love toward us, in that, while we were yet sinners, Christ died for us.' That is what we need: a gospel that will have something to say to us when we realize what a poor business we have made of trying to follow the Sermon on the Mount and the teaching of our Master. Then we need His Cross. Then we need the forgiving redeeming love of God. If we try to do without that, we miss a great part of the fulness of the blessing of the gospel.

Kagawa tries to live out the Golden Rule. Yes, but he doesn't think that is the whole gospel. Listen to this sentence of Kagawa's: 'The formula is the Golden Rule plus the Blood of Christ.'

(3) *Don't forget His victory.* I believe that is another element we often leave out of the gospel; and yet it would hardly be a gospel at all without that. A great many Christian people do miss the fulness of the blessing of the gospel of Christ by being very earnest without being glad and confident and victorious, without ever expecting to be more than conquerors. It is almost as if they thought the Crucifixion was the end of the story. Don't we often make that mistake, as regards the whole tone and temper of our Christian lives? But we never find Christ's early followers in the New Testament feeling like that. They were glad. They thought of Christ as a triumphant Victor, and they knew they would be victorious too. 'Thanks be to God, which giveth us the victory through our Lord Jesus Christ.' And that is the true note of Christianity.

A short time ago I was looking at a replica of Michelangelo's great sculpture, *The Risen Christ.* The Cross is there all right. But Christ is not nailed to it in the agony of death. That is all past now. He is standing on the ground, standing upright, with the Cross beside Him, and His right arm is around it. He is victorious. That is the ultimate spirit of Christianity.

We Christians ought to have something of the note of victory and confidence, calm strength and joy and gladness. Let us all claim that great heritage. It is the crowning glory of a Christian life. I don't believe it always comes all at once. But it ought to come. We shouldn't be content to go on without it. Life ought to become better and richer and gladder for us every year we live if we are Christ's people—yes, even amid all our troubles, because we have our share in the victory of the Lord Jesus Christ.

16. THE WEEPING KINGS

And David went up by the ascent of the mount of Olives, and wept as he went up.   2 SAMUEL 15.30

And when Jesus was come near, he beheld the city, and wept over it.
                                                                            LUKE 19.41

THESE two pictures happened at almost exactly the same spot, though there was a thousand years between them.

There is hardly any more moving story in the Old Testament than the story of how Absalom, the prince, stole the hearts of the people away from his father, King David, and then started a great conspiracy, marching on Jerusalem to seize the throne. When David heard it, he and his faithful followers began to make a hasty trek out of the city, as the only chance of safety. And then, when the city was fairly left behind for the charming traitor to enter with his treacherous crowds, 'David went up by the ascent of the mount of Olives, and wept as he went up.'

And there, a thousand years later, on that same spot, though riding in the other direction, was Jesus. He was surrounded by the shouts of people hailing Him with Hosanna as their King. But He saw pretty clearly that Jerusalem was going to reject Him and even kill Him. As the procession came round the bend of the road, on the shoulder of the Mount of Olives (travellers tell us about the exact spot), the wonderful beloved city came into view. And, says Luke, when Jesus saw it, He wept. Again the people saw their King in tears.

The latter scene is our Palm Sunday subject. But the other scene is so movingly like it, and yet so strikingly different from it, that it will touch our imaginations, and make us see something of the glory of Jesus as He moved on towards the Cross.

(1) *Jesus wept, not for Himself, but for Jerusalem.* David, too, loved the city with a pathetic love and he, too, in that sad hour showed that in his heart there was room for thoughts of other people. There is a very noble kingly touch in the story. And even if he was most of all sorry for himself, can we wonder at that? He might well weep for himself. But Jesus wept for Jerusalem.

Of course that is entirely in line with what we find throughout that last terrible week of the Passion of Jesus, and we must see it if we are to understand His Cross at all: He went to meet it with a heart of heroic love, self-forgetting love. He was not a sorry victim, looking round for pity and breaking down emotionally among His followers.

We remember how, the very last night, when the shadow of death was on Him, He was so obviously thinking more of the disciples than of Himself. There they were, still quarrelling about the chief place; and so (John tells us) Jesus took a basin and a towel and washed their feet, so as to give them something to remember that would teach them a nobler attitude one to another. We remember how in those terrifying hours of darkness in Gethsemane He kept counselling them to watch and pray lest they should be overtaken unawares by the great ordeal. We remember how, when on His very way to the place of crucifixion He saw the women weeping for Him in the streets, He said: 'Don't weep for me, but for yourselves and your children.' We remember how, when in the midst of His agony on the Cross, He saw the rough ignorant soldiers who had nailed Him on it standing around and tossing for His clothes, He asked God to forgive them.

We know too well that we are far sorrier for ourselves than for other people, and sometimes so sorry for ourselves that our neighbours have to bear their burdens alone, so far as we are concerned. But Jesus kept on loving even through the lonely tragedy of His Passion. And that is half the meaning of the Cross. It is not just that He suffered and died (countless others have done that). It is because He went through it with a heart that wept for others and not for itself. That is why the Cross of Jesus is a revelation of the very best and highest kind of thing we could ever try to be, and also above all a revelation of the great loving heart of God.

(2) *Jesus wept, but He went on.* The two processions are going in different directions: the one up the hill, away from Jerusalem, the other down the hill towards Jerusalem. Of course we are not blaming David. No doubt what he did was the best thing to do. But Jesus—He was a different kind of King, with a different kind of Kingdom, which could never be saved by turning back from danger, but only by going on to the Cross.

> We may not count her armies, we may not see her king,
> Her fortress is a faithful heart, her pride is suffering.

That was Christ's Kingdom; and so He did not ride up the hill out of danger, but down the hill, with a faithful heart.

It is very important to remember, when we are thinking of the Cross of Jesus, that all the time He could have turned back. When He saw the danger coming, long before this, He could quite easily have saved all the trouble by giving up saying and doing the things He did, retiring into private life again. Nothing would have pleased the authorities better and Jesus could have finished His days peacefully in Nazareth. Even in Gethsemane, when the band of His captors was drawing nearer, He might (as Dr Glover has pointed out) have escaped: a few hours' walking would have put Him out of danger. But He went on to the Cross, because, come what might, He had to be valiant for truth and for God, and do His appointed task.

Thus it was not only love to man; it was also obedience to God and to truth and to duty. That is why the New Testament in one place describes the glory of it by saying that Jesus became 'obedient even unto death, yea, the death of the cross'. It is the greatest act of obedience in the history of the world.

There are times in most lives when the path of duty is quite plain, but terribly hard to take. In these times we are all prone to substitute self-pity for obedience. But no tears can change the path of duty; and no life can be right that doesn't learn obedience to it. And where can we learn that better than from Jesus, who set His face steadfastly to go to Jerusalem?

(3) *He wept, but He trusted in God.* If one were to ask which is the greatest passage about faith in the New Testament, or indeed in the world's literature, the answer would at once be the eleventh chapter of Hebrews, how by faith one man did this, and by faith another man did that. And the long and eloquent passage comes to a climax by telling us that the supreme and outstanding example of faith in the whole history of the world was Jesus Christ. And what is the reason the writer gives, the thing he mentions that Jesus did by faith? Well, it was this—the way He faced the Cross.

In the story of David, too, there was faith, though it was of rather a desperate kind. 'Take the ark of God back to the city. If I find favour with the Lord, he will bring me back to let me see the ark and its abode; but if he says, "I take no pleasure in you," then here I am, let him do to me as he thinks best.' That was noble, wasn't it? It was religious. He committed himself to God as he fled.

We can hardly read the words without thinking of the triumphant faith of Jesus Christ a thousand years after, when on the very eve of His crucifixion He cried to God, 'My

Father, if it be possible, let this cup pass from me: nevertheless not as I will, but as thou wilt.' What was before Him looked like the black night of ghastly failure and complete tragedy —the end of everything He had ever cared for, all He had ever believed in. And yet He trusted absolutely in God. And so Jesus was already victor, with the victory of faith. As He rode along that road, weeping, to the city that was going to crucify Him, it was not really, in the light of eternity and of faith, inappropriate that the people around Him should be shouting Hosannah, spreading their garments on the road, and waving the green branches of victory. Risking everything for God, trusting utterly in God—it was what He had always taught men to do, whenever He spoke of faith; and now in the last terrible crisis He did it Himself; and it is the greatest act of faith in the history of the world.

It has been the great source and secret of faith for every-body else ever since—the Cross of Jesus. It is terribly hard amid all the tragedies and contradictions and mysteries of this world to believe and trust in an eternal Purpose of good. But there is One who through nineteen long centuries has supremely helped people to do it, and just because of the way in which He faced the greatest tragedy of all.

17. THE SIFTING OF MEN

Satan hath desired to have you, that he may sift you as wheat.
LUKE 22.31

I HAVE been reading recently a very remarkable book, the *Last Journals* of Captain Robert Scott, who died on his way back from the South Pole in 1912. It contains one passage which is the best possible introduction to our subject. Scott speaks of how a great perilous enterprise like his sorts men out and shows their true qualities. 'I do not think there can be any life quite so demonstrative of character as that which we had on these expeditions. One sees a remarkable reassortment of values. Under ordinary conditions it is so easy to carry a point with a little bounce; self-assertion is a mask which covers many a weakness. As a rule we have neither the time nor the desire to look beneath it, and so it is that commonly we accept people on their own valuation. Here the outward show is nothing, it is the inward purpose that counts. So the "gods" dwindle and the humble supplant them. Pretence is useless.' And so Scott goes on to sketch the qualities of one man after another in the expedition. There wasn't one that really showed up badly, because they were all picked men. But they did get *reassorted* by that great testing experience. There were terrible hardships, and all sorts of unexpected emergencies; and so it inevitably became quite plain who were the most unselfish men, who were the most resourceful and reliable, who were the bravest, who were the biggest in heart and mind; and so on. That great perilous enterprise, throwing them all together for so long amid great hardships, sorted them out, sifted them out, showed what they really were, more than twenty years of conventional life at home would have done. And it even does one good and searches one out to read the story of it.

Well, the same thing is true, in a still greater degree, of another story, a greater story—the story of the life of Jesus Christ on earth, moving on through the days and months to the Crucifixion. Those people who were living in Palestine alongside of Jesus were living through the greatest episode in the whole history of the world, though they didn't know it, and all the time it was sorting them out, sifting them out. Jesus here says that the disciples were being sifted like wheat, but it was true of all the people. This wonderful thing going on among them, this great enterprise which also ended in a tragic death—it showed them all up, reassorted them in the queerest ways, and pretence was no use at all. It damaged *some* people's reputations, it gave other people a new chance, it searched out everybody, even the best, to sift them like wheat. That was one side of the whole wonderful story.

And that is one of the ways in which it does us good to read the story today: it searches us out, and banishes pretence, and wipes out some of the lines we draw, and draws fresh lines, and seems to group us quite differently from our conventional groupings. It sifts us out like wheat.

Let us look at some of the groups around Jesus Christ in the Gospel story, and see how they come out of the test.

(1) There were *the people of high reputation*. That is to say, the leaders and pillars of the Jewish Church: the Scribes, who were such students of the Bible; the Pharisees, who were so strictly religious, such lovers of the synagogue; the priests and elders of Jerusalem; or as we might put it in modern terms—the ministers and elders and deacons and theologians and important people of the Church. These people were looked up to in all the country—self-respecting, careful, circumspect, very particular about the company they kept, and about all the pious customs with which religion was

hedged about in those days. No one could have a word to
say against *them*, they could hold their heads high anywhere,
and you would think they would come safely through any
test.

But when this great test came—when they were confronted with Jesus—they came through the test very badly
indeed. They showed up in the poorest, meanest, ugliest
way. For the most part, they couldn't see anything admirable
in Jesus, and He couldn't see much that was admirable in
them. The Pharisees were earnest, serious-minded men,
according to their own standards. But somehow, when Jesus
appeared among them, their goodness began to look very
superficial and unreal. And Jesus told them so. They were
very particular about the conventionalities of religion, but
that was only covering up their lack of real faith and courage
and mercy and love and truth. And, worst of all, when that
began to be shown up, they turned like a pack of wolves
on Jesus, and had a good deal to do with sending Him to
the Cross. They must save their *own* reputation at all costs
—that was what they instinctively thought of: not truth and
right, but the safety of their own reputations. How they
showed themselves by that! And it was much the same with
the priests and Sadducees and elders of Jerusalem. They had
their comfortable honourable position, and their first in-
stinctive thought about this Galilean preacher was that His
movement might unsettle things and threaten their positions.
It was safety first, and their own skins first, whoever else
might have to suffer for it. And so Jesus had to go, and they
got Him crucified. I wonder if it was much the same with
Pontius Pilate the Roman procurator: he also had his reputation and his popularity to think of, and so he didn't venture
to go against those Jewish leaders and do justice to Jesus: he
must think of himself. It isn't a pretty story of all those
people of high reputation showing up in that way. They

didn't realize how they were being unconsciously judged by the demands of a great situation. But there it was; and the respectable folk, the Church-folk (as we would call them) came out of it worst of all.

I always think we Church-folk don't realize that as clearly as we ought when we read the Gospels. We don't realize that those Scribes and Pharisees, whom we so glibly condemn, were the leading Church-folk of the day; and that their spiritual danger was just the kind of spiritual danger to which we Church-folk are always exposed, though *we* belong to Christ's own Church. Are we quite sure that we wouldn't have taken the kind of attitude they took when Jesus appeared among them, a Galilean working-man, without any credentials, upsetting many things? It is good for us to ask ourselves these questions, humbly, honestly, just because we are the people of good reputation.

(2) *The people of no reputation.* That was another of the groups—the groups that you see shifting on that stage of the drama of the Gospel story.

Isn't it curious how that little phrase is scattered all over the page of the Gospel story—'publicans and sinners'? It gives you the situation at once: alongside of the good Church-folk, there were a good many others who were outsiders as regards religion and morality, people who had not kept themselves as they ought. They might be rich or they might be poor; but, from the point of view of the Church, they were 'down-and-out'. They had gone off the track, made a mess of their lives, lost their characters, forfeited the company of the good folk, and indeed all the promises of their religion. They were given their place quite plainly by respectable public opinion, and it was the place of an outsider. They were people of no reputation, and that was an end of them.

But that was not an end of them for Jesus. Jesus was

tremendously interested in these people. That is why they appear so often in the pages of the Gospel: not because there were more outcasts and sinners in Galilee than in other countries, but because somehow when Jesus came into the picture these outsiders came into the picture again too. That was one of the strange reassortments that began to take place. Somehow these people were no longer outsiders. Jesus had something to say to them, and they were strangely responsive to Jesus. Jesus saw something in them—something that no one else saw, and something that He didn't see in the holy Pharisees. Somehow, the sinners came out of the test better. It was not that Jesus made light of their sins—no, they *had* made a mess of their lives, and Jesus was profoundly sorry for them. But He was more than sorry: He was strangely hopeful about them. He looked upon them as lost sons and daughters of God, who could be brought back; and He did help many of them to get back. And so some of the best and joyfullest reading in the Gospels is not about the holy Scribes and Pharisees and elders, of whom you would have expected high things, but about outcasts like Zacchaeus and the fallen woman who came into Simon the Pharisee's house, and all the other broken people who gathered around Jesus and listened to Him and were emboldened to make a new beginning with His wonderful help.

Now isn't that another thing that it is good for us Church-folk to see and realize? In that great time of testing, when God's revelation in Jesus Christ was having strange reactions on different people, reassorting them, sifting them out, showing what they really were, none of its effects was more manifest or notable than this: how it brought the outcast-sinners back into the picture and gave them a new chance, a fresh start. Perhaps the righteous folk *needed* it just as much, only they didn't want to admit that by *taking* it. But the publicans and sinners took it. And that was how the great episode of the appearance of Jesus sorted people out, and sorts them out still: on the one hand there gathers a group of the people who thank God complacently that they are better than their neighbours and don't need repentance and so never get much better; and on the other hand the people— all sorts of people—who are never too proud or too bitter or too cowardly to make a new beginning, a fresh start— thinking not of their own reputation, good or bad, but casting themselves on the pardoning love of God in the spirit of the Gospel of Jesus.

(3) We come to *the disciples themselves*, the third group. And in a sense this was a company of picked men, just as was Captain Scott's company. These were the twelve men that Jesus had picked for His great enterprise. And how did they come out of the great sifting?

At first sight they may seem to have come out of it pretty badly, especially when you come to the final crisis of the Cross. One of them actually turned traitor before the end, and sold his Master. Another lost his courage and his head so completely as to repudiate his Master when he was cornered about it. And every one of them ran away when their Master was arrested. It doesn't sound very creditable. They had been very bold when no danger was near, especially Peter; but when danger came near, these also thought first of their own skins. Not one single man had the courage to go through with it except Jesus Himself: He was left alone, deserted. What a discreditable sifting-out it was!

But, friends, before we condemn those disciples, let us remember how we ourselves are being sorted out and sifted out in the same way every day, and how we play our Master false with far less excuse. Do you never play the coward and the weakling—not in emergencies of great and terrifying danger such as threatened the disciples, but in infinitely less difficult situations—because you are afraid of unpopularity or of ridicule or of something else that is disagreeable; because you instinctively think first of yourself and your own skin, and you would rather let a brother down or let a cause down than take any risks for yourself? Yes, life is sorting us all out in that way, and it takes far less to frighten and vanquish most of *us* than it took to shake those disciples.

Ah, but there is a better thing than that to remember about them. For, though the last tragic episode of the arrest and crucifixion of their Master did shake their loyalty, there was better stuff in them too, and it came out very soon in face of even graver danger. 'Simon,' said Jesus, 'Satan has wished to have you disciples, to sift you out like wheat. But I have prayed for *you*, Simon, that your faith may not fail; and when you have turned again, strengthen your brethren.' And that was what happened. Look at the book of Acts. There you see the authorities out against the Jesus-movement as much as ever; and now the disciples know better than ever what terrible danger they are in. Jesus had actually been crucified, and the authorities might go just as far again. It was a matter of life and death. And they know that now better than ever. But they are calm and strong and brave, valiant for truth, sure of their ground and afraid of nobody— only peasants and fishermen for the most part, and yet not afraid of officials and authorities and courts of justice. The authorities themselves were struck by it. 'When they saw the boldness of Peter and John, and perceived that they were unlearned and ignorant men, they marvelled. And they took knowledge of them, that they had been with Jesus.'

Well, isn't that just the secret? That *was*, after all, the group that came best out of the great tragic hour: the group of men who had been with Jesus. Picked men, to begin with, no doubt; and yet really all sorts of men, a very mixed crowd, that had never been grouped together until they got grouped around Jesus. Some of them had been Church-folk;

some had been outsiders. Some were ordinary working men; one was a wretched publican; one was a revolutionary fanatic, Simon the Zealot; and if there wasn't a Pharisee among the twelve, yet very soon after, when the danger was at its hottest, a leader of the Pharisees did join their ranks, captivated by Jesus Christ—his name was Saul or Paul. That was the mixed group that showed up so nobly, so loyally, so bravely. And if you had asked how they had done it, they would have said it was all through Jesus Christ. He had prayed for them (as this text says), and He had prayed with them, and had taught them and led them and moulded them, and accustomed them to trustful fellowship with their Heavenly Father. He had given them new chances, fresh starts. His very Cross had spoken to them of God's forgiving love and grace, which can bring new beginnings even out of tragedy and failure. And now they are true men. That is what He has made of them.

Friends, *we* are Christ's disciples: a very mixed crowd too, not very valiant, not very stable. But the main question is whether we are letting the Gospel of Christ make true men and women of us as the days go by: through daily repentance and forgiveness and new beginnings; through daily discipline and discipleship; through daily setting our faces to go with Jesus to Jerusalem; through daily victory over little temptations, by the grace of God.

Captain Scott was proud to think that he had with him a company of men who could go through the terrible tests of a Polar expedition like *British men*. Christ needs, here and there and everywhere, men and women who can go through the ordinary tests of ordinary days as sons and daughters of God.

18. THE RELIGIOUS LIFE

And in the morning, rising up a great while before day, he went out, and departed into a solitary place, and there prayed. MARK 1.35

IT is told that just before the Battle of Edghill in 1642 General Sir Jacob Astley prayed with his army the following simple prayer: *O Lord, thou knowest how busy we must be this day: if we forget thee, do not thou forget us; for Christ's sake. Amen.* That, I think, is a good parable of how the religious life has to be lived amid the hustle and bustle of a workaday world.

And now here is another prayer illustrating the same thing, by a man with a very different kind of occupation. It was Dr Thomas Arnold, the famous Headmaster of Rugby School a century ago, who used this prayer every day regularly: *O Lord, we have a busy world around us. Eye, ear and thought will be needed for all our work to be done in the world. Now, ere we again enter upon it on the morrow, we would commit eye, ear and thought to Thee. Do Thou bless them and keep their work Thine, that as through Thy natural laws our hearts beat and our blood flows without any thought of ours for them, so our spiritual life may hold on its course at those times when our minds cannot consciously turn to Thee to commit each particular thought to Thy service: hear our prayer for our Redeemer's sake. Amen.*

I think these two little stories set before us very plainly the whole problem of how a man is to be religious when there are so many other things to attend to in this world. How can you be religious all the time? That is the problem. And I think these two stories give us not only the problem but also the solution. The religious life is not a matter of retiring from the world altogether and giving all one's time to the thought of the divine. But it does depend on finding time in our busy lives for the quest of God in prayer—as that general knew and that great schoolmaster also.

Now it is just the same thing that is illustrated in such a clear and beautiful way in the passage I have taken as our text. And in this passage it is the very case of Jesus Christ Himself. It was all true for Him also—for Him who, as we say, lived in the very bosom of the Father, but who also lived amid the world's work and play. Just notice what it is that we find described in this chapter. Jesus had had an exceedingly busy day, from morning till night—in the morning a very straining and exciting time in the synagogue in Capernaum; then, immediately after, a case of sickness to deal with in a private house, the mother-in-law of Simon Peter; and then at evening a whole crowd of people thronging around the door of the house clamouring to be relieved by Jesus. And He did what He could for them. Then it was bedtime and Jesus and His disciples were very ready for it. But when the disciples awoke next morning and looked around for their Master, He was not in the house at all. Long before daybreak He had got up and gone out, when all was quiet. He had needed rest and sleep for His body, but He needed something else too. He needed spiritual refreshment for His soul, and He could only get it in solitary prayer. And so we have to picture Him yonder on the hillside under the waning starlight and the first streaks of dawn, when no one else was abroad, throwing His soul open to the influences of God in meditation and prayer.

The disciples had hardly seen that sort of thing before, and they were rather puzzled by Jesus. Why had He gone out there alone? They went out and found Him. They said to Him, 'All the people are looking for you.' And He said: 'I must go on into the next towns and preach there also; for that was why I came forth.' And so there was another day opening out before Him. It was going to be busy and noisy, people would be crowding around Him. Eye and ear and thought would be occupied. But through the noise and dust and distraction of it all Jesus would be living as in God's presence, His spiritual life holding on its course, because in those quiet hours of the early morning He had turned His soul to God upon the lone hillside.

There in the perfect religious life you have the picture of the alternation of leisure and work, prayer and activity, the eternal and the temporal. That is how the religious life can be lived in this workaday world.

Now I want in the light of all that to lay down two simple truths about it.

(1) *The religious life does not mean that you will be thinking about religion all the time.* That is impossible. There are plenty of other things in this world that need to be attended to. We all have our work to do, and we have to be thinking of that most of the time—unless we are thinking of it we shall not do it very well. General Astley had to fight his battle. Dr Arnold had to teach his school. Everyone has his task to perform. Jesus Christ had His mission to carry out amid the dust and toil of those towns of Galilee; and even He couldn't be directly thinking of religion all the time.

Now of course there have always been in this world some people who thought that you couldn't be really religious unless you retired from the world altogether into a life of holy seclusion. One can quite well understand that idea and how it has sometimes appealed to enthusiastic souls. Religion seems such a sublime spiritual unearthly thing, and so exacting in its demands, that you haven't very much chance of getting deep into it unless you give all your time to the pursuit of it, without any secular occupation or interest at all. So some people have felt. And thus, with a longing for the religious life, they have forsaken the world and become monks or nuns and lived apart from ordinary mankind that they might live nearer to God. That sort of thing can be seen throughout the course of religious history.

It would be a poor thing for us to condemn all that; for that monastic life has throughout the Christian centuries produced a great many real saints, and has given to the world hymns and books of devotion that will never be forgotten. And yet somehow we can't help feeling that that cloistered or hermit kind of Christianity is very different from the kind of life lived by Christ our Master. He lived a busy human life among the haunts of men. There were, indeed, in His time, as in every other time, good men who retired like hermits from the world. There was John the Baptist, for whom Jesus had such an admiration. John lived in the wilderness. He preached to the people indeed, but they had to go out to the wilderness to hear him. He lived a strange ascetic life, clothed in camel's hair, eating locusts and wild honey—a quite different life from what his ordinary fellow creatures were living in the towns and villages of Galilee.

But Jesus lived among men, moved about among them and shared in their activities, their social joys and sorrows; going as a guest to all sorts of houses, taking part in wedding feasts, carrying on His beneficent work in their towns and villages; so that people even used to contrast Him with John the Baptist, and to say that this Jesus was everybody's companion. He had many things to think of, many people to talk to, much distraction, much occupation for ear and eye and lip and mind. And it was in these circumstances that He lived the perfect religious life. He was living the eternal life amid the things of time.

That is, I say, the real lesson of the religious life. We know that we have to love the Lord our God with all our heart and soul and strength and mind. But that does not mean that we are to be interested in nothing else. That does not mean that we are to be thinking of religion all the time. Nothing could be falser than that idea. For the main thing is not to be thinking about religion, but to be living it. That is the real thing we have to learn, to live constantly in a religious spirit amid the common tasks and distractions and social intercourse of daily life in this workaday world. When we can do that, then we have the happiness of being religious men and women.

It is rather a notable thing that even that Catholic Church of the Middle Ages which gave such honour to the monastic life has so many beautiful stories that teach us that the un-selfish active life among men is somehow best of all. Do you remember the story of St. Basil and the Gooseherd? St. Basil was one of the pillar-saints. He lived day and night for many years on the broad top of a stone pillar forty feet high, praying for his own sins and the sins of the world. Then one night an angel came to him, took him down to the ground and said: 'Follow this road to the third milestone, and there you will find a man who can instruct you, because he is well-pleasing to God.' When Basil got to the third milestone he saw nothing but a flock of geese approaching, herded by a rustic man with a little girl. Basil told him he had been sent to him by an angel for his soul's good. But the gooseherd didn't know what he meant. He had spent his life herding the geese and taking care of the little girl, an orphan whom he had found. That is all the story. And that was the man from whom the holy St. Basil of the Pillar had to learn the secret of the religious life.

Friends, these stories must be welcome truth to us. For we have to live in a workaday world and carry on our common occupations. Of course we can't be always thinking about religion. But we can live the religious life through all our occupations if the right spirit is in our hearts.

(2) *The religious life does depend on your having certain times for meditation and prayer.* It can't be that all the time; it is not

I

desirable that it should be; it is into the workaday world that we have to bring the atmosphere of the divine. But we can't bring it into the workaday world unless we sometimes steal aside from the noise and toil and ascend the mountains of the spirit to breathe the atmosphere of the divine. That was what the general did before his battle. That was what Dr Arnold did before his day in school. They couldn't be thinking of God all the day through their exacting tasks. But they could think of Him and pray to Him at the beginning of the day: and that would set them right at the start and keep them right all through. That is what religious men and women have always done, until almost as a matter of course it has become part of the religious life. And that is what Jesus did too. Indeed I suppose Jesus is the original pattern of that kind of thing in religion—at least in the matter of private prayer. In His time religion was pretty much a public matter. To go off in the early morning to a quiet hillside spot for prayer seemed to the disciples such a novel thing. I suppose the reason why Jesus chose the hillside was partly because no privacy or solitude was possible in one of those tiny village houses of the Galilean peasants, and partly perhaps because Jesus found it easier to lift up His heart to God in the open air and under the open sky, for He was a lover of nature. But the reason why He did the thing at all was because He knew by experience that without that way of beginning the day, without that periodic interval of devotion, it is impossible to keep on living in a religious spirit amid the distractions of the world.

Now that has in the Christian era become a regular part of the religious life. But, after all, how easily it slips out of the religious life—at least out of many lives that profess to be religious and dimly mean to be so! It seems such an idle thing in this busy world to stop and give any time to a matter like the cultivation of the spiritual life. It is so easy to go upon one's way and tell oneself that work is as good as prayer and duty is the best religion and so on, until one has really become weary and worldly at heart without knowing it; just through losing the sense of divine things by the neglect of the spiritual life. For one does soon lose the sense of divine things. It is impossible to keep it, it is impossible to carry the atmosphere of God with one through the common days of toil and care, unless we sometimes stop to breathe that atmosphere in the quietness of a moment of devotion.

Friends, I am sure there are many lives into which a new beauty and inspiration would come if they would only learn to make a habit of that kind, a personal habit of religious devotion. And I am sure there are many homes (even Christian homes) into which a new beauty would enter if they would only revive something of the Christian custom of family worship which is not as common in Scotland as it used to be. What a difference it might make for your whole day if every morning your thoughts and prayers did for a moment turn to God! And what a difference it might make to the whole life of your home if every day there were heard in it, read aloud in the presence of all the household together, the words of a chapter of Scripture, psalm or prophecy, or the wonderful words of our Master in the Gospels.

Don't you think that then in our towns there would be more of the atmosphere which Jesus carried about with Him through the towns and villages of Galilee long ago?

19. THE PARABLE OF THE LOOKING-GLASS

*For if anyone is a hearer of the word, and not a doer, he is like unto a
man beholding his natural face in a glass; for he beholdeth himself, and
goeth away, and straightway forgetteth what manner of man he was.
But he that looketh into the perfect law of liberty, and so continueth,
being not a hearer that forgetteth, but a doer that worketh, this man shall
be blessed in his doing.* JAMES 1.23-25

HERE we have a parable of the looking-glass. And the idea
is that in spite of the looking-glass some people don't know
what they really look like. James says that a man looks in
the glass and sees his face and then goes off and forgets—
doesn't really learn to see himself as he is.

There is a good illustration of that in Charlotte Bronte's
novel *Villette*. The heroine, Lucy Snowe, who was rather an
insignificant-looking person, tells that one evening she was
walking with two friends through the long wide corridor of
a concert-hall when on turning a corner she saw a group of
three people approaching to meet them. And then, after the
fraction of a moment, she realized that she was looking at a
mirror and it was herself with her two friends that she was
seeing. It gave her an unpleasant jar—it was not very
flattering. She had not realized that she looked like that;
though, as she said, 'it might have been worse'. For the only
time in her life she saw herself for a moment as others saw
her. All that is very true to life. We don't usually see ourselves as others see us, in spite of the looking-glass.

Now that is what James takes as a parable. If it is true in
the natural world, it is also true in the spiritual world. There
also we need a mirror, a looking-glass, that will help us to
see ourselves as we are. And we can find it in different forms,
in the Bible and all sorts of other books that can awaken our

consciences. It is extraordinarily difficult for us to look steadily and see our own faults and learn the salutary lesson. It is far easier to shut our eyes and forget. But it is far better to see our faults, that we may overcome them and go on to better things, and the people who do that are the truly blessed people. That is how James uses the parable of the looking-glass. 'If any man is a hearer of the word, and not a doer, he is like unto a man beholding his natural face in a glass; for he beholdeth himself, and goeth away, and straight-way forgetteth what sort of man he was. But he that looketh into the perfect law of liberty, and so continueth, being not a hearer that forgetteth, but a doer that worketh, this man shall be blest in his doing.'

(1) First, then, *think of the looking-glass*, this moral and spiritual mirror that we need. Where can we find it?

We can find it to some extent in many books—in many a novel, especially those that have the element of social satire. According to Hamlet, the purpose of stage-plays is 'to hold the mirror up to nature'. Many a novelist like Dickens and Thackeray and George Eliot, and in our own time many a writer like John Galsworthy, Bernard Shaw, and Sinclair Lewis hold up a mirror to society and to our human nature, in which the sins of the generation are reflected, the sins of one class or another, one type or another. They are not always pleasant reading, but they may be salutary reading, showing us our own sins. We should be thankful for them.

But it is above all the Bible that can hold up the mirror to our consciences. You remember the story of David and Nathan. David had been guilty of a terrible sin, a very mean cruel dastardly action. And he was quite happy about it. He did not see it in all its wickedness, because it had been done by himself, and he was blind with self-esteem. He needed a mirror to be held up before him. And the prophet Nathan supplied one, in the form of a story. He told King

David a story of a rich man who wronged a poor man by seizing his one ewe-lamb. When David heard that story his heart burned with hot indignation, and he said, 'That man must be put to death.' And then Nathan said, 'You are the man.' It was just like what David had done himself. What a good way Nathan took of showing him! It was like holding up a mirror to him, and when David cried out in disgust at the features of the man he saw in the mirror, the prophet said: 'It's yourself.'

At many points the Bible ought to be to us that kind of mirror. Especially, perhaps, the Gospels. When we read of how the different kinds of people reacted to Jesus, the Pharisees and the priests and the common people, and of how their sins of pride and jealousy and cowardice and fickleness sent Jesus to the Cross, we should not complacently pass judgment on these people, but should allow the story to pass judgment on us, because our sins are just the same as theirs. We ought to see our own faults and follies reflected in that looking-glass of the Word of God. We need it.

(2) *How difficult it is to learn the lesson from that looking-glass!* How prone we are, as James here puts it, to look, and then look away, and forget and to go on without repentance, no better than before.

I mentioned Galsworthy's novels a moment ago. Now his books about the Forsyte family are powerful satires on modern life. Soames Forsyte, the 'man of property', is painted as a successful worldly type of business man, highly respectable, but with no heart for anything save material success. I once remarked to a friend that in city life there must be many men like Soames Forsyte, and that it must be very good for them thus to see their picture in a book. My friend replied that probably the real Soames Forsytes never recognize their own portrait in the book; they read it quite complacently, not realizing that they look like that, and thus not learning the lesson of the looking-glass. That is probably very true. Dickens used to find the same thing. He put into his books many ridiculous and unattractive characters, drawn from real life. Sometimes they seem a little overdrawn. Sometimes people used to go to Dickens and tell him that such and such a character in his latest novel was not in the least true to life, that it was quite impossible, and that such an absurd character never existed. And Dickens said that it was usually a person of that type that made the complaint. They themselves were living examples of the type that they thought impossible, and they didn't see it. They didn't recognize themselves in the glass.

And how easy it is to read the Bible in that blind way, and apply its judgments to other people, not to ourselves. We read in the Gospels our Lord's denunciation of the Pharisees for religious hypocrisy and make-believe and self-righteousness, and we complacently say, Amen! But we don't feel convicted of any of these qualities ourselves, and the very fact that we don't shows that we are self-righteous! We read the story of the rich young man who couldn't bring himself to make an act of renunciation in order to follow Jesus and we say he made 'the great refusal'. But we don't ask ourselves whether we would ever have dreamt of doing what Jesus asked him to do. And probably our lives show that we wouldn't. We read of Peter denying his Master, and we call it moral cowardice, and we don't notice that we are constantly showing such moral cowardice as regards our own Christian witness in the modern world.

Even when we do apply these ancient lessons to present-day life, we apply them censoriously to other people, not to ourselves. I'm sure that is one of the great spiritual dangers of an age of crisis. We may be sure that God has much to say to our consciences through the dreadful events of this age; and our reading of the Bible ought to be helping us humbly to hear it, and penitently to accept God's judgment. But we let God judge only our enemies, not ourselves. We condemn the evil things we see in them, and quite rightly. But surely Christianity, the Christian witness in our land, should have something more to say on such matters than public opinion generally—something for our own consciences. All the evil things that we have rightly condemned in our enemies, all the false gods that have brought the world to its present wretched pass, selfish nationalism, prejudice against the Jews and other forms of race prejudice, worship of the material, secularism, apostasy from Christianity, from the Christian faith or from Christian moral standards—have we no share in these evils? Haven't we gone after strange gods? And isn't it a dangerous thing to say that in the crisis of these recent years God has been judging our enemies, but not ourselves? If we do that, then the evil things against which we have been fighting may continue to live on undefeated in our own national life and in our own hearts. That is the tragedy that always happens when we refuse to be penitent and to take God's judgment home to ourselves. 'If any man is a hearer of the word, and not a doer, he is like a man who sees his face in a glass and goes off and forgets what sort of man he was.' That is how people lose their souls.

(3) But, *there is the promise to those who look and learn.* 'But he that looketh into the perfect law of liberty, and so continueth, being not a hearer that forgetteth, but a doer that worketh, that man shall be blessed in his doing.'

That is given as an announcement of the wholesome Christian way of living. What does it mean? Why does James speak of looking into 'the perfect law of liberty'? What kind of looking-glass is that? He seems to mean (as we can gather from another passage in the next chapter, where he repeats the phrase 'the law of liberty')—he means just the Christian Gospel, which is different from the old Jewish Law. The Gospel has a liberating effect, because it leads beyond judgment to mercy, to repentance and forgiveness, release from the past and a new beginning.

This Epistle of James does not always seem to be a very evangelical epistle, and it is well known that Martin Luther was not very fond of it—it did not seem to preach the gospel of justification by faith. Yet it does really point us beyond mere morality to the liberating message of the mercy of God. And that is what is so vitally important. It is immensely important to realize that the Christian way of life is not simply to see ourselves as we are, to see our faults and concentrate on overcoming them, to set our teeth and doggedly cultivate our characters and so save our souls. That method is not successful; it does not make good Christians, but, at the best, self-righteous Pharisees. The Christian way always is to look beyond our own sins to the grace and mercy of God in Christ. The Gospel is a looking-glass which reflects not only our own miserable selves, but also the glory and love of God. And if we continue (as our text says) looking into that glass, we come to be set free from ourselves and grow into the Christian character. It is just what St. Paul says about the looking-glass: 'Beholding as in a glass the glory of the Lord, we become changed into the same image.' And it is just what St. John says (though he doesn't mention the looking-glass): 'If we say we have no sin, we deceive ourselves, and the truth is not in us': we never come to know ourselves. But 'if we confess our sins, he is faithful and just to forgive us our sins, and to cleanse us from all unrighteousness.' That is the perfect law of liberty, the Gospel that sets us free.

Now this leads us to a very simple and practical conclusion. There is a daily discipline of the Christian life, in which a man, enlightened by the reading of God's word, daily confesses his sins, receives God's forgiveness, accepts the grace of a new beginning—and so makes a fresh start every day, by the grace of God. That is what makes up the perseverance of the saints. 'That man,' says our text, 'shall be blessed in his doing.'

Yes, these are the truly blessed people, in this time of judgment or any other time. Not the complacent people, who are content with judging others: they are not blessed. And not the proud moralists, who judge themselves and can never forgive themselves: they are not blessed. But those who every day humbly accept the gifts of the Gospel of Christ, and are daily delivered from themselves into the liberty of the children of God.

20. A MAN'S LIFE

A man's life. LUKE 12.15

I HAVE been asked to speak to you about 'Christ and the Purpose of Life'. He often used to talk about 'a man's life' —that gift which is bestowed upon us all, and which is the most individual thing we have, a life to live, a soul with a short spell of existence in this world between birth and death. That is the one thing we all have, however little else we have, and it is our very own, to make or mar, to use or waste, and it can't be repeated. It is our chance, our opportunity, our life. He said: 'A man's life doesn't consist in the stock of things he possesses.' He said: 'The life is more than the food.' He said: 'What good is it to a man if he should gain the whole world and forfeit his life, lose his own self? Or what should a man give in exchange for his life?' Let us begin by trying to envisage that thing of which Jesus speaks, that gift which is a man's chance, a man's life.

There are certain periods of human life that especially make one think of it and the wonder of it. First of all, when you see a very young baby just beginning to look around him, your imagination is sometimes touched. There is the beginning of a life. That little child is going to be a person distinct from all the other countless millions of persons that have lived on earth. He has life stretching out before him, a life of his own, in a line different from the line of any other life, through childhood, youth, manhood, old age, to death —yes and, we believe, also beyond death on into all eternity. That is what sometimes comes home to us with a sense of wonder as we look on a little child. But again, I believe, sometimes when people stand at the end of their life, they have a vivid sense of the wonder of the thing they have had, the chance which is now past. After all, it won't be very long for any one of us till we stand there, and then, looking back, we shall perhaps see it stand out more wonderful than ever before—this life, this bit of time given to us on earth, this chance we had, which is now past and can never be repeated for us. We'll say: 'I've had my chance, my life is no longer in front of me—it is behind me.' Then again, another period of life when it sometimes comes home to us is in what we call the period of adolescence—the time when a lad or lass is growing up into manhood or womanhood. At that stage there comes a very keen sense of individuality: a young fellow becomes conscious of himself as a man among men, with a life of his own to live, a choice of his own to make. That is the age at which you will find a fellow quoting words like those of the American poet:

> Life is a leaf of paper white,
> Whereon each one of us may write
> His word or two, and then comes night.

So a young fellow thinks the long long thoughts of youth, as he sees his life—'a man's life'—stretching out before him, his very own, to make or mar.

But there is yet another period of life when perhaps more than at any other we get an almost startling vision of the wonder of this chance that is given to us, and are made to ask ourselves questions as to what it is all about and what we are making of it: I mean the middle years, the middle watch, say, round about the forties and after. And perhaps that comes home to most of us more than what I've said about the other periods. I believe it is not an uncommon thing for men and women of that age to waken up, as it were, and realize that they don't know what the purpose of life is, or what they are living for. Hitherto they have moved on in the stream of a busy and successful life, and now they begin

to wonder whether their life can really be described as successful, and whether it is all worth while. I wonder if that
was how it was with the man who wrote the Book of
Ecclesiastes. He aimed at all manner of big things—wealth
and pleasure and learning—and he got them all. And then
he found he didn't care for them, because he didn't know
what it was all about. There wasn't really any purpose in
his life, and he said: 'All is vanity, and a striving after wind.'

There is one very famous example in modern biography.
It is the case of the great Russian novelist, Leo Tolstoy. He
had worked hard at his literary labours, and had won both
wealth and fame, and was happily married. And then, when
he was about half way through his forties, when he might
seem to have all that heart could wish, he suddenly began to
wonder what was the use of it all. It is a very moving story.
He described the thing afterwards in these words: 'Five years
ago a strange condition of mental torpor began to grow
upon me. . . . The same questions continually presented
themselves to me: 'Why?' and 'What afterwards?' . . . my
life had come to a sudden stop. I could breathe, eat, drink,
sleep—indeed I couldn't help doing so. But there was no
real life in me. . . . Life had no meaning for me.' That was
the beginning of the crisis that led to his conversion. Can
anybody read the words without being moved? Don't they
make us ask questions about our own lives?

It seems to me that Jesus used to try to awaken people to
that kind of question, about their lives and the meaning of
life. He saw around Him so many people who simply didn't
realize the wonder of having a life to live. They were far
too easily satisfied. Or at least they thought they were satisfied. They were engrossed in making a living, or in making
a fortune, and by a kind of optical illusion they thought they
were busily engrossed in the main purpose of human life.
But they weren't touching the main purpose of life at all.

They were engrossed in life's mere machinery, making a living, but never asking why they wanted to make a living, what they were going to do with their living when they had made it, never knowing what they were living for. Jesus looked on these people with a profound pity. They were so blind. They were making such a poor thing of life, from every point of view. They weren't even happy. They couldn't even enjoy life in this beautiful world. And as for the purpose of life, they simply weren't making anything of their lives at all. It's a very wonderful thing to have a life to live. It's a big thing. 'The life is more than the food.' 'A man's life doesn't consist in the stock of things he possesses.' That is only the machinery of life, and the people who were engrossed in that weren't really living at all. They were simply losing their lives, throwing away their chance, making the worst of both worlds—too feverish even to enjoy God's material gifts, and missing the eternal purpose of life altogether. How Jesus used to try to open their eyes—to give them a glimpse, even though it should be a terrifying glimpse, of how life was passing away and they were making nothing of it, but just 'losing their own selves'!

It wouldn't be at all a bad thing for many a man or woman to have such a glimpse: to have their eyes suddenly opened, to realize that perhaps half their life is past, or perhaps two thirds of it, and they don't know what they are living for. Thirty-five is about half time, and forty-five is well on in the afternoon, and fifty-five or sixty is towards evening. And twenty is the golden morning. And a man's life is given him only once to live. What are you making of yours?

But now—to move further on—what is the true purpose of life in this world according to Christ? What are we here for, according to Christ? What are we here for, according to the Christian theory? Let us try to get clear about the answer to that—it is so easy to get it wrong and confused. What is the purpose of life?

(1) Is it simply to get our souls saved for heaven? That sounds a very simple answer to the question: that the one thing man should really trouble about during his short span in this world is to make sure that when he dies he will have a straight passage to heaven. One of the greatest of the early Fathers of the Church said: 'The work of a Christian is nothing else than to study how to die.' And perhaps you have sometimes heard that view expressed among modern Christians, and perhaps you have wondered if that was really the whole truth. Of course, there is truth in it, but it isn't the whole truth. That doesn't do justice to the Gospel of Christ at all. He certainly didn't mean anything as narrow and self-centred. He meant something far bigger—I might almost say more reckless—than that. He didn't mean His followers to be continually thinking in a fearful way of death, but rather to be superior to the fear of death. And as for taking care of oneself and one's chances, saving one's life, one's soul—well, He would say that if you try to do that in any selfish timid kind of sense, you will only lose it; and that the only way really to gain and keep and save one's soul, one's chance, is to pour it out, bravely, nobly, unselfishly, lovingly—in fact, to lose it—not to be afraid to lose it. Then you'll find it. That is to say, Jesus called His followers to do something much braver with the chance they have than simply to save it up for themselves. We've got to think of others as much as of ourselves if we are going to learn His secret of life. A man can't save himself alone—because then he wouldn't be saved from selfishness, and if you're not saved from selfishness you're not saved at all in any sense that Christ would care for. What then is the purpose of life according to Jesus?

(2) Is it simply that we should serve our fellows, and

make this world a better place, leave it a little better than we found it? Surely there's truth in that answer. That does remind us of Jesus, and it appeals to all that is chivalrous in us. And yet—does it tell us enough? To serve our fellows, to make this world a better place—well, yes; but better in what way? Simply more comfortable for everybody? But if we've discovered that material comfort is a poor purpose in life for ourselves, how can it be the aim of our life to give more of it to others? And if we haven't really found any big enough purpose to be the end and object of life for ourselves, how can we solve the problem by getting busy in the service of others? We don't know how to serve them. We don't know what we want to give them. It would be just going round and round in a circle, chasing our own tails because we don't know what it's all about. And I'm sure a great many people have made that discovery. Weary of material possessions and ambitions, they have thrown themselves busily into the 'gospel of service', and have found it a weariness because they didn't know what their ultimate purpose was, didn't know what it was all about.

What is it all about, according to Jesus? What is the purpose of life, on His view?

I don't think you can ever answer that question until you bring in the word 'God'. And I don't know that there is any better answer to the question in one sentence than in His own unforgettable words: *Seek first the Kingdom of God.* Let me try to put it all very simply into a paragraph.

The one great reality is God; and the purpose of life is that we should become sons and daughters of God. That is what He has created us for and given us this spell of life on earth for—that we might learn that and grow into it. Every noble impulse we feel within us, urging us to choose what is right even when it is hard, urging us to choose something better and higher than material prosperity—that is God working in us and drawing us to Himself. Every time our hearts go out in pity and help to a fellow creature or to humanity around us—that is God, moving us to find Him in our fellow creatures and to love Him in them. We have to become sons and daughters of His. We can't do it selfishly by ourselves, for to be a son or daughter of God is to love and serve our fellows. But then, on the other hand, we can't really keep on loving and serving our fellows until God has come into the business and we know what it is all about. Let God come in, let Him rule, let His love have its way, seek His Kingdom, His reign of truth and love, stake everything on that. Then you know what life is all about, and it makes everything worth while. It is God that makes all the difference.

Then we may fail, time after time, and feel that we are not worthy to be His sons and daughters. We are poor specimens of humanity. But still there is God, our Father; and He still wants us to be His sons and daughters. That is enough; that makes it worth while; and we can begin again. Time after time we may grow weary of service to our fellows and feel that anything we do can't make much difference in this vast world, so it isn't worth while. But still—there is God: His Kingdom can't fail, and so our little efforts of love and service can't be lost or wasted. He makes them worth while. That is the life to which Jesus calls us, the life for which we were created. In such a life everything falls into its place: the good things of this world fall into their rightful place, and all the beautiful things of God's creation and the joys of this wonderful world; yes, and the sorrows too, and the pains, and all that is hard and strenuous —they all play their part; and as we go through it manfully, serving our fellows and finding God in them, we grow more and more into sons and daughters of His, for time and for eternity.

135

K

That is what 'a man's life' is meant to be. That is what Jesus calls us to. Young men and women, who still have life's chance in front of you, what are you going to do with it?

21. FOLLOW THOU ME

What is that to thee? Follow thou me. JOHN 21.22

THE scene from which these words come has, even more than most scenes in the Gospel, an atmosphere of eternity. There is about it something timeless that takes us into the presence of the Eternal, so that instead of Christ and Simon Peter it might be Christ and you and I today. Every word has a kind of universal and eternal meaning. And yet also every word has a special reference to the personality and history of Simon Peter; and that is where we must begin.

Everybody knows the Simon Peter who comes so often into the Gospel story in the New Testament. But everybody doesn't know the other things which are told us about Peter outside of the New Testament in the early traditions of the Church; and one of them is the tradition that long long after this, when he was quite an old man, he laid down his life for his faith, that he was actually crucified as his Master had been (and even that, because he didn't think himself worthy to die just like his Master, he was, by his own request, crucified with his head down). That was what Peter came to in the end. Now, though Peter's crucifixion is never definitely related in the New Testament, yet the shadow of his cross falls plainly upon this passage.

Christ says to Peter, 'When you were young, you girded yourself and went wherever you liked.' Well, that was so like the young Simon Peter. When he first became a follower of Christ, he was impulsive, independent, strongheaded, sometimes jibbing against authority, and liking to take his own way. 'But', Christ goes on, 'when you are old, you will stretch forth your hands, and somebody else will gird

137

you and carry you where you don't want to go.' When he
came to be an old man, he would be dependent on other
people and at their mercy. Yes, but there is more in the words
than that. In his old age Peter was to stretch out his hands
on a cross, and be girded with cords and carried to the place
of crucifixion as a martyr for Christ. There is a foreshadowing of that in the scene between Christ and His young disciple. And then immediately Christ goes on and says to
Peter, 'Follow me.' Peter hesitates, Peter trembles and looks
aside, and he sees another disciple, the Beloved Disciple,
standing by; and Peter tries to put Christ off by asking a
question. He says, 'Lord, and what about this man? What
is going to happen to him?' And Christ gives him an answer
which means just this: 'Never you mind about him.' 'What
is that to thee? Follow thou me.' These are the words I have
taken as text. You may have one kind of lot in this life of
discipleship and he may have another; and you may be
puzzled by that, and may want to ask all sorts of questions
about it, and about God's will, and all the mystery of the
crosses of this life. But you can't expect to answer all these
questions, and that is not the main thing. The main thing is
loyal discipleship. 'What is that to thee? Follow thou me.'

You can understand why I began by saying that whatever
the scene meant when the chapter was written, it has an
eternal and timeless quality; and it speaks to our very hearts
amid all our questionings about the great realities of Christ's
Kingdom. 'What is that to thee? Follow thou me.' Let me
try to translate that challenge in three different ways that
will fit ourselves.

(1) *Never mind your perplexities, but follow Christ.* There
is many a young heart which, when it hears Christ's challenge,
does just the thing that Peter does in that scene—begins to
ask questions: 'What about this, and what about that? There
are all sorts of problems I can't solve, and how can I follow

Christ until I become surer about these things? How can I follow Him until I've got my doubts disposed of?' Many a one has spoken or thought like that.

Now sometimes these perplexities are not genuine perplexities at all, but merely excuses, convenient evasions, a sort of red herring drawn across the trail, because it is far easier to raise questions and difficulties than to rise up and follow Christ. When you don't want to live according to God's will and to listen to His voice, it is rather convenient to begin to doubt His existence, to raise the question how we can be sure that there is any God at all. I haven't any doubt that in some cases that is what lies behind people's so-called perplexities. But what a terrible thing that is! That is just a case of admitting into your soul the worst kind of lie, and if you are doing that, what you need is not argument about your questionings, but to get rid at once of the lie in your soul and to face the question whether you are prepared to live up to the best you know and do what you know to be right.

With many people, however, it is not that low dishonest kind of questioning, but very genuine doubt and perplexity about the truths of religion. Many young people pass through that discipline, and those who have been through it know very well what a painful desolating experience it is—to want and long to believe in God and to build one's life on religion, and yet to be tormented with perplexity and uncertainty as to whether it really is all true. Now what can be said to a man in that situation? Well, of course, you have to face your doubts and perplexities quite frankly and honestly and try to think them out and get light on them. But the great and salutary and reassuring lesson is this: that it is not just by thinking it all out that light comes, and that you don't have to wait until you have thought it all out (or you would have to wait forever). You can go on bravely in the path of duty and purity and love. That must be right—you are sure enough of that. So much of Christ is plain to you, and so far you can follow Him with your eyes wide open. And that is how further light comes. 'He that doeth the truth cometh to the light.' Christ doesn't demand all sorts of elaborate beliefs before you can begin to follow Him— that was not like Christ at all. And if you are perplexed about this and that, Christ says: 'What is that to thee? Follow thou me.'

Do you remember the answer Principal Shairp of St. Andrews gave to the perplexities of last century about religion? He put both the question and the answer in poetry.

> I have a life with Christ to live,
> I have a death in Christ to die,
> And must I wait till science give
> All doubts a full reply?

And then his answer:

> Nay, rather, while the sea of doubt
> Is raging wildly round about
> Questioning of life and death and sin,
> Let me but creep within
> Thy fold, O Christ, and at Thy feet
> Take but the lowest seat;
> And hear thine awful voice repeat
> In gentlest accents, heavenly sweet:
> 'Come unto me and rest:
> Believe me and be blest.'

In that sense, I say, never mind your perplexities, but follow Christ: not in the sense of burking your questions and closing your eyes (no, Christ wouldn't force anybody's faith or call anyone to evade their perplexities)—but in the sense of following His light as far as you see it; and everyone can see enough of it to call them, even amid their doubts, to a better, nobler, braver, cleaner, kinder life. Everyone can hear that call 'Follow thou me.'

(2) *Never mind what other people are doing, but follow Christ.*
In this vivid scene, when Peter is challenged to follow Christ,
he begins to talk about the other disciple. There is something
so straight and personal about Christ's challenge: why
shouldn't the other disciple have as hard a challenge? Why
should he get off—what about him? There is something so
lonely about this business of making up his own mind to
follow Christ: why couldn't he be sure of having the other
disciple with him? He wants to wait for that. 'What about
this man?' he says to Jesus. But Jesus replies: 'What is that
to thee? Follow thou me.' It reminds us of Luke's story of
how a man once asked Jesus: 'Is it a small number that will
be saved?' Jesus replied just this: 'You strive to enter in at
the straight gate.' Never mind what other people are doing,
but follow Christ.

There are many ways in which people still try to evade
Christ's challenge by looking at other people. Some do it
by criticizing other people—pointing at the faults of Christians, pointing at the misdeeds and hypocrisies of people
who profess to be Christ's followers, and making that an
excuse for not following Christ themselves. I wouldn't like
to be the kind of Christian who by his unchristian way of
living has the effect of turning other people away from Christ.
God save us all from that! Jesus said it would be better for a
man to be tied to a stone and drowned than to live to make
young people stumble. But did Jesus say that that excuses
anybody for turning from Him because of other people's
faults? No, He would say: 'What is that to thee? Follow
thou me.' And with all your excuses and criticisms of other
people, you know in your heart that Jesus was right.

Then there are some who hesitate about following Christ
wholeheartedly because they do want company, they don't
want to make a lonely choice, or to go further than their
friends and comrades. They want to know how far other

people are going to go in this great Christian business, before they commit themselves. 'Lord, and what shall this man do?' asks Simon Peter with a frightened lonely feeling. There is nothing unnatural in wanting human company and comradeship in following Christ. It would be most unnatural to try to do without it. From the very start the Christian life was a life of fellowship. Nobody knew that better than Simon Peter among his friends; and we ought to know it too (I'm going to speak about that in a moment). But behind all that fellowship, and even independent of it, there must be the lonely choice of each one of us. Do you remember how, at the beginning of *The Pilgrim's Progress*, when Christian became concerned about fleeing from the City of Destruction, his own family and friends gave him no sympathy or understanding or encouragement in the matter? They scolded him about it, and laughed at him, and cold-shouldered him—did everything they could to dissuade him. And then he made up his mind for himself, and set out alone on the pilgrimage. He made good friends and comrades on the way, but he started out with a lonely choice. I hope none of us will have to do it in such a lonely way as that; but it is important that we should hear Christ's call for ourselves and obey. So I say to you all, and especially to those of you who are young: never mind what other people are doing, but follow Christ.

(3) *Don't be merely a member of the Church, but be a follower of Christ.* Now there is nothing on earth greater than the Church. It is part of the very essence of the Gospel. Its fellowship is near the heart of the Christian life. The Christian life was never meant to be a lonely business. It was meant to be a life of rich warm comradeship—the comradeship of the Church. Thank God for that. And yet, it is quite possible to be 'churchy' without being truly religious or Christian. 'Churchianity' is not Christianity. And we

are sometimes in danger of confusing them. Yes, aren't we Church folk sometimes apt to try to satisfy ourselves with religion as a pleasant social institution, that never goes deeper than human fellowship? And even the good works we do in the service of the Church—don't we sometimes perform them merely in a spirit of busy good-fellowship, to please somebody or other, to keep the machinery humming merrily? And the result is that we miss even the deepest kind of human fellowship (there is far too little of that in the Church) because we don't go deep enough to get it. Real deep Christian fellowship only comes when people are united in this supernatural enterprise—discipleship to Jesus Christ.

I've already quoted one St. Andrews Principal, J. C. Shairp. Let me now quote another, a still greater, Samuel Rutherford, whose grave is one of the glories of St. Andrews Cathedral graveyard. When Samuel Rutherford lay on his deathbed in 1661, some of his brother ministers were gathered around him and he spoke to them of Christ. 'Dear brethren,' he said, 'do all for Him; pray for Christ, preach for Christ, feed the flock committed to your charge for Christ; do all for Christ. Beware of men-pleasing; there is too much of it among us.'

Isn't that a sound message still for all Church-folk, whether ministers or people? Do all for Christ. Go deeper than all human fellowship, deeper than all mere churchmanship, listen to the voice of God in Christ, and do all for Him. 'What is that to thee? Follow thou me.'

My friends, what would the Church of Christ in all the ages have been without that? What would the Church in our own dear land in past generations have been without that—without that kind of thing happening in the lives of all sorts and conditions of men and women, in cottage and castle, up and down Scotland?

143

And if the Church is going to be a true live Church of Christ in Scotland in this coming day and generation, it will be because its men and women, like you and me, and above all because its young men and women, growing up out of childhood, hear for themselves the call of Christ, and rise up to follow Him.

LECTURES

1. WHAT IS DEAD AND WHAT IS LIVING IN CHRISTIANITY

I

'WHAT is dead and what is living in Christianity?' The words may be taken to imply that we have to pick and choose; that some parts of the Christian message are true, and some are false, and that we have to pick out the true elements and assemble them and make a religion out of them. They might even be taken to suggest that we have to pick and choose what is true in the various religions of mankind, separating it from what is false and transient, and then, by an eclectic and syncretistic process, make a composite religion which would include what we have chosen as true from Christianity. Now, I will not for a moment deny that the Christian theologian may learn much from the study of non-Christian religions. But I do not believe that it is by an eclectic and syncretistic process that he will learn it. And even apart from the widespread net of a syncretistic process, I do not believe that the Christian religion can be regarded as a collection of doctrines which may be treated eclectically, so that some shall be taken and others left. Christianity is an organic whole.

I remember reading many years ago a remark of the great English literary critic George Saintsbury (one of my old teachers) which stuck in my memory and is relevant to my present point. He was talking of the religious heresies of Matthew Arnold, and he said something like this: that they all sprang from the fundamental heresy which he had inherited from his father (the notable Dr Thomas Arnold of Rugby), that one can pick and choose, accepting certain

elements in the Christian creed and rejecting others. According to Saintsbury, that was the fount and origin of all heresies and all errors.

Now when I first read that, many years ago, I did not agree with it or with its implications. But I think I have come to understand better what Saintsbury meant, and to see in it a most important truth. There *is* a unity and wholeness about the Christian message. It does stand for a simple integrated view of God and man and the world. Each part of it implies and is implied by the other parts; so that there is a very profound sense in which it is impossible to pick and choose, to add and subtract, to cut off some doctrines and try to engraft others, without destroying what a Scottish theologian has called 'the organism of Christian truth'.

I should like to try to illustrate what I mean by some concrete examples.

Some years ago I was giving an address to students about some aspects of Christian belief, in particular the Christian belief in 'the life everlasting' beyond death. When at the close of my address it came to question-time, one student asked the following question (I do not profess to remember the exact words): 'What about the doctrine of reincarnation, the transmigration of souls into other bodies through a succession of lives after this life is past: Does not that sound a reasonable doctrine, and could we not take that doctrine and graft it into the Christian religion in place of the traditional Christian belief in what lies beyond the grave?' What is the answer to that question? I believe the answer is (and I said something of this kind at the time), that the doctrine of transmigration and reincarnation of souls belongs to an entirely different religious outlook from the Christian outlook, and that the two could not possibly mix. The doctrine of transmigration and reincarnation belongs to a Hindu world of thought, which regards individual existence as evil,

and regards desire as evil; so that the true purpose of life is the suppression of all desire, in order that we may get rid of Kharma as soon as possible, in order that instead of having a long series of reincarnations after this life, we may escape as soon as possible from our personal existence into Nirvana. Quite apart from any scientific difficulties about the conception, it does not make sense at all when tacked on to the Christian religion. It does not fit. It belongs to a totally different world-view. And the Christian world-view demands its own eschatology, which in its turn is unintelligible unless we read it as the final chapter of the Christian story. In that sense the Christian faith is a single organism, and cannot be broken up.

It will be worth our while to look a little longer at this matter of Christian eschatology in relation to the whole of Christian belief. It is important to realize that Christian eschatology is quite a different thing from a theory of 'the immortality of the soul'. Strictly speaking, the idea of the immortality of the soul is a Greek and Platonic idea, and was not part of the original Christian message at all. It is true that it did infiltrate into Christian teaching through the influence of Greek philosophy, but it never fitted in very well, and it always remained but a subordinate part of a whole eschatology which spoke of death and resurrection rather than of immortality. There is a very notable contrast at this point between the Greek Platonic idea and the outlook of the New Testament. The Platonic doctrine does not take *death* very seriously, at least does not regard it as an evil and an enemy, but rather as a release, by which the immortal soul is set free from the prison-house of the body, that it may live its own untrammelled life. But the New Testament does regard death as an evil and an enemy. It is 'the last enemy', though an enemy that has been overcome by Christ. And it does not speak of the immortality of the *soul*,

as if the body were evil and godless and therefore unimportant and perishable, while the soul is immortal. Nay, the Bible never makes that false dualism between body and soul which modern philosophy is beginning to repudiate. Man is a body-soul organism, and the body as much as the soul is part of him as created by God. The body is not in itself evil or godless, and the soul is not immune against death. This whole body-soul organism, which has somehow fallen away from God, is subject to the dreadful crisis of death. But God can rescue it from death through Jesus Christ: and the result of this is not 'the immortality of the soul', but the resurrection of the whole person from death to eternal life.

That is the authentic Christian doctrine. No doubt it needs some interpretation today (and I may return to that matter); but it cannot be simply interchanged with the Platonic conception. The Platonic conception does not fit into the whole scheme of Christian belief about God and man and body and spirit; whereas the Christian doctrine of eternal life is an integral part of a whole Christian theology and anthropology and eschatology. In the modern world people are sometimes disposed to suggest that it would be a good thing to drop from the Creed the words, 'I believe in ... the resurrection of the body.' We certainly do not believe that these bodies of flesh and blood, which are laid in the grave and decay, will one day literally rise out of their graves. And yet it would be foolish to drop the words and to substitute 'I believe in the immortality of the soul'; because what Christianity believes in is not the survival of a ghost set free from its mortal body, but the resurrection of a personality by the power of God, who made all things, visible and invisible, body and soul. And without this, Christianity makes no sense.

This leads me to another illustration of the principle I am laying down. A moment ago I spoke of 'God who made

all things, visible and invisible'. That is the Christian doctrine of Creation. Or, to put it in a still more distinctive form: 'God made all things out of nothing.' *Creatio ex nihilo*: that is a distinctively Christian idea. But does it mean any thing in the modern world? Is it not merely an ancient and primitive and pre-scientific way of answering the question of origins? Must we not replace it in the modern world by something rather in the nature of *evolution*? That is a question that many will ask. And they will suggest that the doctrine of creation is part of the dead wood that may be cut away from the Christian faith, which can live all the better without it in the modern world. To many people that will seem to be an obvious point at which we can distinguish between what is dead and what is living in Christianity.

But again I am quite sure that they are wrong. The Christian doctrine of Creation—of *creatio ex nihilo*—is not a primitive pre-scientific theory of origins which has to give way to the concept of evolution. It is not in any way inconsistent with the scientific theory of evolution. But it moves at a deeper level, it deals with a more ultimate question, and it says something which is quite basic to the Christian faith and makes a vital difference to every part of it. The doctrine of Creation out of nothing steers a path between pantheism on the one hand and radical dualism on the other—on the one hand, the pantheistic idea that the world is an emanation from God's own substance and is ultimately indistinguishable from God; on the other hand, the idea of God making the world out of an already existent raw material, which exists independently of God. That latter gives you a Manichaean dualism, which regards matter and the body as evil and godless, over against God. Both of these opposite views, pantheism and radical dualism, are quite incompatible with Christianity. If you adopt either of these positions, you cannot have the Christian attitude to God as infinite, or the

Christian conception of man, or the Christian ethic of the body, or the Christian idea of Incarnation, or the Christian doctrine of resurrection and immortality. And therefore Christianity says: God did not make the world as an emanation from Himself; nor did He manufacture it out of some independent raw material. He created it out of nothing. Doubtless that sounds paradoxical if you try to treat it as a scientific theorem. Perhaps it is something which can only be expressed in semi-mythical form. But it stands for a perfectly clear issue in rejecting pantheism and radical dualism and steering a path between them. And thus it says something that is vital to Christianity. You cannot have Christianity without the Christian doctrine of Creation.

These are all illustrations of my thesis that it is impossible to distinguish what is living and what is dead in Christianity by selecting some doctrines and dropping others. You cannot do that, because of the unity of 'the organism of Christian truth'.

II

I will now briefly discuss *another* way of trying to make that distinction. It is what I may roughly call the Hegelian method. It consists in dropping the historical element in the Creeds and reducing Christianity to a system of eternal timeless truths. This method does not pick and choose between the doctrines, retaining some and dropping others. It keeps all the doctrines of Christianity, recognizing that they form an organism. It keeps them all, *but with a difference*. It regards the historical element in them as having only a symbolical value. They symbolize eternal truths about God and man. Ultimate truths must always be metaphysical. Religion is a pictorial or imaginative way of expressing truths which can be more exactly and correctly stated in philosophical or metaphysical terms. And so when Christianity as a religion makes historical statements (as in the Creeds), the historical element must be taken only as a symbolical way of expressing certain philosophical truths. Thus the central Christian doctrine of the Incarnation must not be taken as making stupendous affirmations about a man called Jesus who lived in Palestine long ago and was a divine-human person, but must rather be taken as symbolizing the eternal truth of the unity of God and Man.

This is what I have roughly designated the Hegelian way of trying to separate what is dead from what is living in Christianity. It came to its clearest expression in what we may call the 'Hegelians of the left'; and its most famous and extreme exponent is David Friedrich Strauss. As a New Testament critic Strauss dissolved away a very large part of the Gospel story into legend. But on his theory that was no particular loss, because what matters is not the historical fact but the timeless truth which it symbolizes about God and Man. So the actually historical reference can be dropped, and the whole system of the Christian doctrine retained in its purely symbolical sense.

It seems clear that this again is a false way of making a distinction between what is dead and what is living in Christianity. For Christianity in its very essence is an historical religion, and if you cut out the historical element, it is no longer Christianity. In this connection it is significant that Strauss himself, while he began by presenting a new version of Christianity set free from historical fact, ended by giving up all profession of Christianity in favour of a religion of humanity. Surely it is not accidental that the Christian Creeds contain an historical element. It might indeed be said that the authentic Christian message is not a system of time-less truths, but a story, and (as I like to put it) *a story with a plot*. It is true that the early chapters of the story (about Creation, Fall, etc.) go back beyond history altogether into a supra-historical realm of which we can only speak in symbols. And the final chapters of the story, lying in the future, belong also to another world of which we can only speak pictorially. But the central part of the story is firmly nailed down to history on this planet (running through your life and mine), and the very central chapter tells of an episode that took place nineteen centuries ago in Palestine 'under Pontius Pilate' as the Creed says. Other religions besides Christianity have had a sacred story attached to their cultus, but it did not matter to them whether the story was historically true. Professor Clement Webb of Oxford wrote, concerning Greek religion: 'So long as the ancient ceremonies were observed, so long as the cock was sacrificed to Aesculapius, it mattered but little whether one were orthodox with respect to the truth of the stories which were told respecting Aesculapius.'[1] But Christianity is bound to take its historical element seriously, as *history*, not mere symbol. The whole Christian conception of God and of His relation to the world, and of the relation of time and eternity, is bound up with this. Christianity does not believe in a God whose interests are remote from human affairs; nor does it believe that eternity means mere timelessness, nor that time is an illusion, nor that the visible world is an illusion and history does not matter. Christianity believes in what the Bible calls 'the living God', a God who 'does things', who is interested in history and works in history, a God who creates and reveals and redeems. Therefore Christianity must 'take time seriously', and must say things not only about what God *is*, but about what He *does* and *has done*—what He did on the hard soil of terrestrial history 'under Pontius Pilate'. Without that historical reference, Christianity could not utter its message at all.

[1] C. C. J. Webb, *Studies in the History of Natural Theology*, pp. 23-32.

III

I should like now to speak very briefly of yet another way in which the attempt is being made in our own time to distinguish between what is living and what is dead in Christianity. I am thinking of the idea of the *Entmythologisierung*, demythologizing, of Christianity, about which controversy has been raging in theological circles on the Continent of Europe for some years. It was all started by Professor Rudolf Bultmann, of the University of Marburg in Germany, one of the most distinguished New Testament scholars in the world. In a work published some years ago Bultmann contended that it is necessary to free Christianity from its mythological element if it is to be made intelligible to the man of today. According to Bultmann, the whole world-view of the New Testament is a mythical world-view. It speaks in terms of a three-storey universe. The top storey is heaven, where dwell God and the angels. The bottom storey is the underworld, containing hell and the powers of evil, the Devil and his hosts. The middle storey is this earth, which is the scene of human history. And the whole Christian message in the New Testament is couched in terms of that mythological three-storey universe. Both the powers of heaven from above and the powers of hell from below extend their action to this middle storey, and contend with each other for the life of man. God comes down to earth to redeem man, and redeemed man rises from the power of death and goes to heaven. It is all stated in those mythical terms. And thus it is wholly unintelligible to the men of today. For modern man does not think of the world in those mythological terms. His world is quite different. And therefore if the Christian message is to get across at all to the man of today, there must be *interpretation*; and the interpretation must take the form of *Entmythologisierung*, demythologizing.

It must be restated in non-mythical terms. And how can that be done?

Bultmann's answer is virtually that the Christian message must be restated in *existentialist* terms. Bultmann has, I believe, been influenced by the existentialist philosophy of Heidegger and Jaspers, and so to him the vital need is that man should come to have a true understanding of his own existence. And this is what Christianity can give him. It is into these terms that the Christian mythology has to be interpreted. When the New Testament tells us that we are in the grip of the powers of evil, but that God sent His Son down into this world to liberate us, it is really telling us that what is wrong with all of us is our proud sinful independence, from which we cannot save ourselves, and that the one thing that can liberate us from it is the message of God's forgiving love revealed to us in Jesus—not so much in 'the Jesus of history' as in the New Testament message of the saving death and resurrection of Christ. That saves us from ourselves, and that is the real message of Christianity when translated out of 'mythological' into 'existentialist' forms.

What shall we say to this attempt to 'demythologize' Christianity? Many theologians have agreed that Bultmann has drawn attention to a genuine and urgent problem—that of interpreting Christianity to the man of today. But very diverse criticisms have been offered. One distinguished Swedish theologian, Bishop Nygren, has suggested that, while it is indeed difficult for modern man to understand the New Testament message, the real trouble lies not in the myths of the New Testament, but in the myths of the modern mind; for example, the myth of extreme individualism in its conception of human nature, which makes it very difficult for us today to understand the New Testament conceptions of corporate sin and corporate salvation ('As in

Adam all die, so in Christ shall all be made alive'). We are beginning to see that this individualistic way of regarding human life is far from watertight, and this is the beginning of a sound demythologizing, not of the New Testament message, but of ourselves.

Others have suggested that the aim of demythologizing is really a false and futile aim, since we cannot dispense with myth and mythological forms in our statements about ultimate realities—and I think there is a great deal of truth in that contention, though some will prefer to speak of *symbolism* rather than of mythology. If we are to go beyond mere analysis of our own existence, if we are to have any objective content in our Christian doctrines, if we are to speak of God and the unseen world of heaven, and the future life therein, and God's purposes and God's acts in history, we are bound to speak in highly symbolical terms, with spatial metaphors, with the application to God of verbs in past, present and future tenses, though we know that He 'inhabits eternity'. We must not try to translate these symbolical expressions into purely conceptual terms (like the Hegelians), for such realities cannot be expressed in purely conceptual terms. I have a great deal of sympathy with the religious existentialism which tells us that 'God cannot be expressed but can only be addressed' (Buber). Divine realities can only be known in a personal 'I—and—Thou' relationship. They cannot be the object of disinterested objective conceptual knowledge. When we try to conceptualize them, we fall into contradictions—and therefore we are bound to use symbolical expressions, pictorial accounts, which convey their meaning only to those who take the existential 'I-and-Thou' attitude of faith. For that reason it seems impossible to distinguish between what is living and what is dead in Christianity by the simple method of demythologizing. For that procedure goes on the too easy assumption that all symbolical expressions are 'mythological' in some *bad* sense, and therefore must be eliminated.

IV

Is there, then, no answer that we can give to the question: What is dead and what is living in Christianity? When we there say 'dead' and 'living', do we mean 'false' and 'true'? Or are we merely making a distinction between elements in the Christian message which in this particular age in which we live are actively believed and those which are ignored or dropped? In *that* sense, may there not be certain beliefs which are dead at present, but which will come to life again in a future generation? Can't we think of certain Christian beliefs which were almost dead half-a-century ago, but which have come alive again in our time? A great part of Christian eschatology had been dropped or was being very much soft-pedalled in the Christianity of fifty years ago, and yet has come right into the centre of Christian thinking again in our times. Indeed, it might be said that all the new discussion in our time of the meaning of history, the Christian interpretation of history, is largely due to the rediscovery of eschatology in the message of the New Testament. Another example is the conception of Original Sin. Fifty years ago this was certainly not a living idea in theological circles, and it might have been thought that Christianity had finally dropped it as dead wood. But it has become vastly important again—I need only remind you of the writings of Reinhold Niebuhr (not to mention T. E. Hulme's *Speculations*, outside theological circles altogether).

Of course these ideas are being re-interpreted. That is the constant task of theology in every age. In the theology of past ages—every past age—there is a great deal that is dead and will doubtless never come to life again, though it is always dangerous to make such sweeping predictions. Doubtless there is much in the theology of the present age which will be dead fifty years hence. For the task of theology is never complete. It has to be done over again in every age. It is being rethought all the time. This does not mean that it is getting further and further away from the thought-world of the Bible. As a matter of fact the rejuvenescence of theology in our own time, with its many new insights, is largely due to a kind of rediscovery of the Bible, a new understanding and appreciation of Biblical Theology. This does not, of course, mean anything like a return to the idea of an infallible book, verbally inspired, as a compendium of religious doctrine, or a repudiation of all the new light thrown upon the nature and structure of the Bible by modern historical criticism, but a further stage, which gives us a still richer way of using the Bible, and which has greatly affected the ever-changing shape of theology. Of course there are many things in the many theologies of the past that do not satisfy us; just as there are certainly many things in our present-day theology that will not satisfy our grand-children. Thus the task of theology has to be undertaken over and over again; while the central content of faith remains the same. It is only in that sense, as it seems to me, that we can safely and humbly make the distinction between what is dead and what is living in Christianity.

23. CAN JESUS BE BOTH GOD AND MAN?

A GREAT many people have quite mistaken ideas about what Christianity has always meant in saying that Jesus Christ is God, or that God was incarnate in Jesus, or that God became man; and I must begin by clearing away these misunderstandings.

Suppose that when Jesus lived on earth someone had seen Him walking along the street and asked a bystander, 'Who is that man over there?', do you think it would have been correct to answer: 'That is not a man, that is God'? Of course nobody would have dreamt of giving such an answer. And it would have been quite wrong. For Jesus *was* a man, and to start by saying He wasn't would have been to make a false start. But could it also be said that He was God? That certainly would have been very puzzling. For if you had followed Him along the street and heard Him talk to the people, you would have heard Him speaking *about* God in the third person. If you had waited, you might even have heard Him praying to God, speaking *to* God, in the second person. But how then could He *be* God? Would it be better to say that He began by being a man and grew into a God through sheer goodness? No, indeed. That is not what Christianity has ever meant. Or perhaps that He was a man while He was on earth, but He became a God after His death? We know that He was put to death by crucifixion, and we can't say that *God* died on the Cross, for God can't die; so perhaps you think Christianity teaches that Jesus died as a man but then He was exalted and became a God. But that is all wrong. And indeed it is misleading to talk about *a* God at all, as if the word 'God' were a common noun which could have the indefinite article before it, and which could have a plural. There is only one God, and there couldn't be more than one. The very word 'God', in the Christian sense, is a proper name. And it is all wrong to think of Jesus as a kind of second God alongside God the Father Almighty.

It is quite true that Christians speak of God the Father, God the Son, and God the Holy Spirit. That is an attempt to express something which cannot be perfectly expressed in any human language. But Christians have never meant that these are three gods, but that these three are one God. And as regards Jesus, this is what Christians have been trying to say: that God was incarnate in Him, and yet the life of God was not confined to what was seen in the life of Jesus. God is infinitely great, beyond our understanding; and though He has shown us in Christ as much as we could understand, yet the *whole* life of God *could* not be shown in a human life on earth. So Christians have said that it was not God the Father, but God the Son, or the Son of God, or (to use another term) the Word of God, that was incarnate in Jesus. 'The Word became flesh.' Or, to put it in its simplest form, God became Man.

I said 'simplest'. But it is not exactly simple. What does it mean? Does it mean that at a certain point of time God *changed* into a man? No, certainly it does not mean anything as crude as that. That would be like the stories of 'metamorphosis' that you find in ancient classical mythology. But God does not *change*. And in any case what Christians believe about Christ is not that He changed from being God into being a man, so that He was *first* the one and *then* the other, in succession; but that He is *at the same time* both God and Man.

Does that mean that Jesus was a kind of demigod, an intermediate being, between God and man, half and half, like the demigods we read of in ancient Greek literature? No, indeed. That is a pagan idea, and it would make Jesus quite unreal, for then He would be neither God nor man, but a strange mythological figure. What Christians believe is that He is *both* God and man. But does that mean that His mind was divine and His body human? Was it just a case of God inhabiting a human body for a period of thirty years? No, indeed. That again is a pagan idea, like the stories we find in classical legend of some god appearing on earth for a short time in human disguise. That is not real incarnation at all. We Christians believe that not only Jesus' body, but His *mind*, was truly human, that it really worked like a human mind, because it was a human mind. And this last point is so important that we must look at it a little more closely.

The whole life of Jesus on earth becomes unreal to us unless we understand that it was truly a *human* life. Jesus was first a baby, then a boy, then a man. When He was a boy, He had to learn things gradually as other boys had to do. And when He was a man, he knew no more in scientific and historical matters than other men of His time. He did not know in advance, each moment, everything that was going to happen. He often had to go forward, as it were, in the dark, walking by faith, and it was sometimes very difficult. Even more important, He had to fight real battles against temptation, as all men have to do. They were not sham fights, but real conflicts, and sometimes terribly hard ones. He was like ourselves in everything that is truly human, though not in our sinfulness. All that is bad in us is a *perversion* of our humanity. It is not true humanity. And that is where the humanity of Jesus was different from ours. He did not *yield* to temptation, He won His battles. But His life was in the fullest sense the life of a man, with a human body and a human mind.

Yet at the same time, Christians believe, He was truly God, and His life was wholly divine.

But how could He be both together? How could the same life be both completely human and completely divine?

Well, that is the supreme mystery of the Christian faith. I do not think we *can* altogether penetrate that mystery: it is what theologians sometimes call a paradox. But I always find it helpful to remember that this is not the only point in Christian belief where we find that element of mystery and paradox. In fact we find something of it at all the main points of Christian faith. Let me try to explain.

Christians believe that the providence of God covers all our lives at every point. Everything that comes to me, day by day, all the day's events, all the happy things, and also all the things that seem to be mishaps and reverses, come to me in the providence of God, because He knows what I need better than I know myself. And yet at the same time all the things that happen to me happen through ordinary chains of cause and effect, the workings of natural laws around me, and the actions of my fellow men, sometimes even malicious actions. My whole environment is a network of these forces, and on what we may call the *horizontal* level that is what determines my daily fortunes, whether good or bad. And yet there is at the same time what we may call the *vertical* relation to God, who rules over all, and I believe that the day's events come to me from His will. So there seem to be two sides to it all, the divine side and the earthly human side. They are both real, and each of them covers the *whole* area of my life. We can't quite see how, and that is why I call it a paradox. But I think that may help us to see that there may be a paradox, though of a different kind, in the life of Jesus, which was both divine and human.

And here is another paradox which helps us even more. A Christian is usually ready to acknowledge that any good

there is in him is not really his but God's. Of course there is
a great deal of evil even in the best of Christians, and a
Christian accepts full responsibility for that. He knows that
the evil is his own, and he blames himself. And yet when he
does something good he doesn't congratulate himself and
feel proud of it. He says, as St. Paul once said: 'It was not I,
but the grace of God.' He does not mean that he is a kind of
marionette manipulated by God. He knows that he is a free
agent, and that his actions are his own, his free choice. And
yet so far as there is anything good in them, they are *God's*
actions. It was God who enabled him to do them. They
began with God. Indeed a Christian would say that he is at
his freest just when he is most dominated by God. Never
are his actions so truly and fully free and personal and human
as in those moments when they are wrought by God. That
sounds very strange—it *is* a paradox—but it is just what
hosts of Christians have found in their own experience.

Now it seems to me that this can point us to the still
greater paradox which we find in the Incarnation. Here the
paradox covers not merely little bits and pieces of life, iso-
lated actions and fragments of good, but the *whole* life of
Jesus, all that He was and all that He did and said and thought.
In our own case, even the best of us, it is only little fragments
of our life that are good, and all the time they are mixed with
evil. But suppose God should come right into human life,
in the most complete and personal way. How would that
show itself? It would show itself in a life that in every thought
and word and deed was completely covered with the kind
of goodness that comes from God. And that is what we
believe the life of Jesus was. It was, to its very depths, a life
of perfect human goodness. But that is not the whole truth
about it. That is never the whole truth about goodness.
There is a deeper and prior truth. This was not simply Jesus:
it was God. It was the life of God Himself coming into

human life: as the hymn puts it, 'God's presence and His very self, and essence all divine'. And that side comes first, because God always comes first. That is the real meaning of the life of Jesus. That does not make it any less human or less personal. Jesus was more perfectly human and personal than you or I, and His life was in the fullest sense a human life. But its being completely human does not make it less divine. This was the life of God Himself. This was God incarnate.

Now do you see that it makes a great difference if we can really say these things about Jesus? Perhaps you sometimes think that it is too mysterious, and that we ought to be content with saying that Jesus was the perfect Man and the perfect Teacher, and that He can therefore tell us about God better than anyone else. Isn't that enough? Well, Jesus can certainly tell us about God better than any other teacher can —about the God who is our Father, and who calls us to be His children. But is that all we can say—that Jesus tells us *about* God, tells us how to find Him? If that were all, it would seem to imply that God Himself was not doing anything about it, merely waiting for us to find Him. But God is not like that. He doesn't wait, He seeks us, He leaves nothing undone to lead us back to Himself. He comes all the way in quest of us. And so He became incarnate in Jesus, came right into our human life and our human lot. And when Jesus suffered and died on the Cross, God was not just sitting in heaven watching what was happening. God was there, God was in Jesus, bearing the sin and suffering of the world that He might bring men back to Himself. As St. Paul once put it: 'God was in Christ, reconciling the world to Himself.' So when we speak of the Incarnation, when we say that Jesus was both God and man, we are not merely saying something about Jesus: we are saying something about God, and something that makes all the difference in our conception of Him.

Let me try to make that last point still plainer. There is a vast difference between God and man. God is infinite, eternal, omniscient, omnipresent. Man is a very limited being, mortal and fallible, living always in one particular bit of space, because he lives in a body. In one sense we might say that there is an infinite gulf between God and man.

Now, we might ask: On which side of the gulf does Jesus stand? Is He on the human or the divine side of the gulf, on ours or on God's?

The answer is that Jesus is on *both* sides of the gulf. He is certainly on *our* side of it, for He is a real man, a figure in history at a particular time and place, in which He lived a completely human life. And so we can take Him as our example of how human life ought to be lived in this world. As we read the Gospels we ought to try to see Him as He was, in all His humanity, so that we can follow Him. We can, as it were, stand beside Him, and hear Him praying to God, and we can pray *with* Him and through Him. He stands beside us, facing God across the gulf.

Yes, but it is also true to say that He stands facing us from the other side of the gulf, the divine side, and we can hear Him say (as in the New Testament): 'He that has seen me has seen the Father.' And so as we look across the gulf, we can, as it were, look into the eyes of Jesus Christ, and through His eyes God looks at us, and through His lips God speaks to us. So as we look at Jesus, we can say (in the words of St. Thomas the Apostle): 'My Lord and my God.' It might almost be said that the gulf *disappears*, because God has bridged it by becoming incarnate, because Jesus stands on both sides of it, God and man.

24. MAN AND THE UNSEEN WORLD

I CAN imagine somebody exclaiming at the outset: 'What is this unscientific flight of the imagination? Matter we know, and morality we know, and civilization we know, and the social order we know, but what on earth is the unseen world?'

Yet it is only educated and sophisticated man that would ask such a question or profess to be mystified by the title. For here is the impressive fact with which we have to begin: that from the dawn of history and all over the world we do find man conscious of an unseen realm surrounding his life—conscious, that is to say, not only of a physical environment and a social environment, but also of a more mysterious spiritual environment, a realm of the superhuman, the divine, with which, though it is unseen, he has to do. There can be little question about the universality of that conviction. Travellers have indeed sometimes brought back tales of some race of men in some remote quarter of the globe who had no semblance of religious belief or practice, no consciousness of anything corresponding to what we call the divine. But time after time such impressions and reports have been proved mistaken by further and more sympathetic investigation. This or that savage tribe may not possess anything which at first sight looks like religion to an untrained observer with preconceived notions; but the religion is there none the less—some incoherent awareness of a mysterious unseen superhuman world, and some poor attempt to get into friendly relations with it. It certainly cannot be said of unsophisticated man in the mass that 'God is not in all his thoughts'. It may safely be said that there has never been a

race of men on earth that was not conscious in some way of
an unseen world.

That remarkable fact does not indeed *prove* anything, but
it must make any thinking person ask questions. Tonight I
have to try to answer some of those questions, speaking from
the point of view of those who as Christians believe in the
unseen world. The fundamental question is: What accounts
for this conviction, so remarkably universal? Where did
man get it? How did man come to know? Or for that matter
if we ourselves believe in such an unseen divine reality, how
do we know? Or if somebody is uncertain about it, how can
he find out and make sure? How does anybody know that
there is a God, a soul, a Heaven? Let us try to find an answer
to that inevitable question.

I

Some people will be inclined to answer the question quite
simply by the one word 'revelation'. They will say: 'We
know these things because God has told us. We could never
know them unless God had supernaturally revealed them.
But He has; and now we know, by revelation.' Most
Christians would agree with that in one sense or another;
and it would indeed be absurd to think that we could find
out anything about God unless He willed to reveal Himself.
But the word 'revelation', taken by itself, does not answer
all our questions. It rather raises fresh questions. Are we to
confine the word to the revelation transmitted in the Bible,
as has been very widely done among Christians? If so, what
are we to make of the fact with which we began—the fact
that some knowledge of the existence of an unseen world is
found in every race of mankind, far beyond the influence of
the Biblical revelation, sometimes indeed on a very low level,
but sometimes on a surprisingly high level? Yet if we extend
the meaning of 'revelation' to cover all that, then we have

the whole question on our hands again, as to what we *mean* by revelation and how it enters the human mind. And indeed we should in any case have to face that question. How do we recognize and authenticate revelation? What is the human side of revelation? How do we apprehend it? It is that side of the question that we are concerned with in dealing with man and his world. So that we are back at the question with which we started: Why do we believe in the unseen? How do we arrive at our conviction regarding it?

Some people will say that the conviction must be based ultimately on philosophical proof. There is no other reasonable or reliable way of arriving at any such conviction than to base it on scientific or philosophical argument: so they will tell us. Even the beliefs of primitive races regarding an unseen world of spirits around them are based upon their primitive processes of reasoning—primitive science or philosophy endeavouring to account for the existence and nature of things, and arriving at a crude animistic explanation which peoples the universe with mysterious unseen spirits that have to be worshipped or placated because of their superhuman powers. And as for our higher truer conceptions of the divine, these are the result of more enlightened reflection upon the universe. Only by such philosophic thought can man find out authentically about the unseen. That is one view.

I believe that view to be entirely mistaken. As regards primitive races, anthropology is tending to move away from the idea that their religious beliefs and sentiments are based on their animistic philosophy. Their animistic philosophy alone could never give them the kind of unseen world that matters for religion. Why should they worship the unseen merely because it was unseen? How could they know that the unseen was worth trusting or even propitiating? No, it was not primitive philosophy that told them, and it could never tell them, what they needed to know for religion. And neither can enlightened philosophy tell us what we need. It seems to me that philosophy in the modern world is recognizing this. It is realizing that you can't really prove the existence of unseen divine realities by metaphysical argument from natural facts, and that, unless you *start* with some kind of belief in them, philosophy will never take you there at all. That is not at all discreditable to philosophy. But it means that instead of religion being based on philosophy, philosophy at its highest must rather be based on religion.

Thus we may drop the theory that philosophical speculation is the road by which we must proceed if we are to have any well-grounded assurance about the unseen world. And we shall surely be glad to drop it—it savours so much of intellectual snobbery, and it would provide such a melancholy situation for plain unphilosophical people, by leaving them at the mercy of philosophical experts for their deepest and most sacred convictions.

There are others, again, who maintain that our knowledge of the unseen world must be based on spiritualistic communications. That is in these days a fairly widespread view: that the only really reliable evidence of the existence of an unseen spiritual world is the 'spiritualistic' evidence, obtained by getting into touch with the spirits of the departed through specially endowed 'mediums'. I am not going to say anything about the authenticity of the supposed communications (though we must know that there has indubitably been a great deal of imposture), because I am not competent to do so. Nor shall I dwell on the fact that the Christian Church has almost always refused to give its blessing to such practices and arguments, nor discuss the reasons which the Church has offered. It seems to me sufficient in this place to point out that spiritualism at the best could never prove the kind of things which we need to be sure of in our religion, and indeed has very little bearing on them. What we need to know is not that there is a realm of spirits to which the dead pass, but that there is a moral and spiritual purpose at the heart of the universe, a supreme Goodness which we can trust and to which we can entrust our dead. In other words, we need to know that the unseen is trustworthy. There is no special virtue about being merely 'unseen'. The unseen might be more uninteresting or more depressing than the seen. An unseen world might be as bad as a seen one or worse. What we need for religion is a realm which is not only unseen, but moral and spiritual, infinitely good and reliable, worthy of worship and of trust. We need the conviction that behind the whole world of our experience there stands a Purpose and Will of perfect goodness and love, a God whom we can absolutely trust. Have we any reason to think that spiritualistic communications, even if authentic, and even at their best, are likely to help us towards such a conclusion? I cannot see it.

But that word 'trust' brings us much nearer to the answer that we are seeking. Christianity has always maintained that it is neither by philosophical speculation nor by spiritualistic research that we gain our vital knowledge of the unseen world, but by Faith. That is the decisive word—Faith. There is no limit to what we might quote from Christian literature in illustration of that statement. But we need only refer to the classical passage in the eleventh chapter of the Epistle to the Hebrews. 'Faith is the assurance of things hoped for, the proving of things not seen. . . . By faith we understand that the worlds have been formed by the word of God, so that what is seen hath not been made out of the things which do appear. . . . Without faith it is impossible to be well pleasing to him: for he that cometh to God must believe that he exists, and that he is a rewarder of them that seek after him.' And so on. All of which means that what

we really need to know about the unseen is that it is trustworthy, and the only way to know that is by beginning to
trust it and trusting it more and more. The only way is by
trust, or faith.

II

This brings us to the next stage of our argument. For we
can only go on to ask: What *is* this faith which matters so
much? Some indeed will ask that question with considerable
impatience, feeling that the word 'faith' savours of mystifica-
tion and obscurantism. People often imagine that faith means
simply blind acceptance of what is imposed by authority or
tradition, the unconscious irrational tendency of the un-
awakened mind to adopt the opinions that are continually
'suggested' by its social environment. A well-known psycho-
logical writer tells us that what the psychologist calls suggestion is by the clergyman called 'perception by the eye of
faith'. And a great many people imagine that the clergyman's advice to the rank and file of humanity would be
something like this: 'You can't be expected to form any
worthy judgment for yourselves on these deep mysterious
matters: you must have faith to accept what I tell you, to
believe what is prescribed.' But obviously that cannot be
the last word on the question. For in many minds, of the
questioning and doubting kind, there would immediately
arise the further questions: 'How are we to know that the
authority is right? Which of the various conflicting authorities are we to believe? And how does the authority know?
Is it by faith too?' If so, we are not any nearer to an understanding of what faith is. However important authority and
tradition may be in forming the faith of the individual, all
this does not give us any answer to the question how mankind ever apprehends or recognizes religious truth at all. And
in any case, if we were to use the word 'faith' to indicate

merely blind submissive acceptance of prescribed beliefs, we should be doing grave injustice to a word which has played a splendid part in the history of religion for two thousand years.

But if the clergyman really has something better than that to say about the matter, what is it? How would a really wise spiritual counsellor deal with an honest and perplexed doubter who went to him for guidance? If we could answer that question, we should begin to understand what it means to say that it is by faith we know the unseen world. Suppose the doubter says: 'I have lost all my belief in the unseen. I didn't want to lose it. I should be tremendously relieved to get it back. I hope it is all true, but I simply can't feel sure. How can I come to be sure of an unseen world that I can trust, a God to whom I can pray?' What would the wise spiritual director say in reply?

He would not try to *prove* the truth of it all, either by philosophy or by spiritualism, for that is just what we have seen you can never do. He might try to clear the ground by removing some intellectual difficulties or misunderstandings, but that would be only a negative preliminary. His positive approach would be something like this. 'Isn't there *something* you are sure of in the realm of religious conviction —not all the elaboration of Christian dogma, but some deep simple conviction that somehow there is a Purpose in the universe, that goodness is at the heart of things? Don't you feel sure of that? Then hold on to that, and live in the light of it, and that dim trust will grow into all the fullness and richness of Christian faith in God.' But suppose the doubter answered sadly and honestly: 'No, I can't say I have any such basal conviction. I am not prejudiced against it, I would give anything to possess it, but I simply can't feel sure even of that.' What would the spiritual director say then? Here we seem to touch rock-bottom, and if we could answer the question, we should surely see what faith is, stripped of all its draperies and deprived of all its external supports, standing on its own feet, *sola fides*.

I believe this is what a wise counsellor would say (and many a time must it have been said to an honest doubter amid the perplexities of the modern world). He would say: At least you can go ahead in the path of right living. You are quite sure about that. You may question the existence of an unseen world, but when it comes to actual practice you are quite sure of the existence of a moral law with an absolute claim upon your allegiance. 'It must be right to do right,' to choose in daily life what is pure and honest and brave and generous, at all costs. *There* is something you are quite sure of. You can go straight on in that path, whatever are your doubts about what you call the unseen. And if you do, persistently, faithfully, you will gradually come to be sure of something else too. You will come to feel that the voice calling you to these things is not simply your own voice. It is not just the beating of your own heart you are hearing. It is the beating of the heart of the universe. It comes through what you call your own Conscience, yet it is a voice which transcends everything else in the universe. That is what you will gradually recognize.

> So through the thunder comes a human voice,
> Saying, O heart I made, a heart beats here.

In other words, you will come to be sure that those ideals of purity, honesty, courage and love are but the shadowings of an unseen realm in which they are perfectly realized, a Kingdom of Love, nay, a King of Love, a God whom you can absolutely trust. In listening to the voice of what we call by the dull name of Conscience you were really listening to His voice, though you did not know it; and the more you listen and follow, the more you hear those marvellous divine overtones which make mere morality seem such a poor

business and which give you the blessed assurance and reality
and joy of religion, of God.

That is how the unseen world reveals itself to man. That
is what faith is. It is something which *comes*, as a gift from
the unseen, to those who will receive it. 'If any man willeth
to do God's will, he shall know concerning the doctrine.'
'He that doeth the truth cometh to the light.' 'No man hath
seen God at any time: if we love one another, God dwelleth
in us, and his love is perfected in us.' These familiar texts
all tell us of the one way in which the unseen world can be
apprehended by man; and it is the only conceivable way in
which the unseen world *could* reveal itself to man, just
because it is a world of moral and spiritual perfection: it is
the Kingdom of God.

III

Now I believe that from the very beginning of history it
has been in some such way that the unseen world has revealed
itself to man—by making a direct moral claim upon him in
his everyday environment and assuring him of its support as
he responded to the claim. No doubt in primitive savage
peoples there is not much that we should at first sight call
morality. But the rudiments are there, in their tribal customs
and obligations, or man would not be man at all; and these
rudiments are closely bound up with their rudimentary belief
in the unseen. Even primitive man knows that his tribal
loyalties were not laid on him simply by his tribe, but by
the unseen superhuman forces that work in his tribe and
inspire its religion. Thus 'mere morality' is unheard of and
unthinkable in primitive society—it is one of the abstractions
of the sophisticated mind—and to primitive man such
morality as he has is bound up with the unseen world, to
which he can therefore take up an attitude of awe-struck
dependence and trust. As the religion of mankind rose to

higher levels through the centuries, the more prominent and conscious did this element of trust become: faith in a spiritual world which could be counted on to support what was good. Such an element can be traced in the religion of many nations of the ancient world, notably perhaps in Greece and in India. But there was one ancient nation in whose religious life the element of faith or trust appeared with incomparable clearness and strength—the race of Israel. Anyone who knows the Psalter does not need to be told how in Israel religion became a matter of *trust in the unseen* more than it had ever been anywhere before. And so the Christian writer who wrote the classical passage, already cited, in the Epistle to the Hebrews felt that the meaning of faith could not be better illustrated than by a catalogue of the heroes of ancient Israel. About the heroic choice made by Moses he writes: 'By faith he forsook Egypt, not fearing the wrath of the king; for he endured, as seeing the Invisible One.' So the race of Israel learnt to trust the unseen.

That brings us to the climax of the story. For from the race of Israel there eventually sprang One who trusted the Unseen absolutely without limit, and His followers have ever since regarded Him as the pioneer and perfection of faith— Jesus Christ.

If you ask yourself what new religious truth Jesus gave to the world in His teaching, you may find it hard to answer. You may find it difficult to lay your finger on any quite new thing which was never hinted at by prophet or rabbi before Him. Perhaps it is foolish to try. For what He did was something greater and more universal. He took what everybody knew already in the realm of religion, and went the whole way with it. It was neck or nothing. Everybody knew that God was good and that they ought to trust Him. Yet they did not trust Him very far, whenever it came to the pinch. But Jesus said, in effect: God is *absolutely* good:

why don't you trust Him *absolutely*? How often He said that kind of thing to people, amid the troubles and mysteries of life! 'Where is your faith?' 'O you people of little faith.' 'Anything is possible to a man who believes.' To trust the unseen absolutely, because it is Infinite Love—that was the secret of life, according to Jesus. It is all over the Gospel story. Moreover that was not only what He taught: that was what He *did*. As a well-known theologian of our time has put it: 'For the first time in history there appeared on earth one who absolutely trusted the Unseen.' Thus the unseen, the divine, came breaking through into His life as it had never done before in the life of humanity. It has made an immeasurable difference ever since to people who wished to know the unseen. It has made faith immeasurably easier and surer. It has given faith an incomparable rallying-point: not only a superlative case of human faith in the unseen, but at the same time, and *ipso facto*, a superlative *revelation* of the unseen, vouchsafed by God to man. If revelation were our subject we should dwell upon that aspect of the matter, which is indeed the deeper and prior aspect. But though our subject is rather the human side of the process, we cannot draw to a close without remembering that the unseen God of Christian faith is a God who does not wait to be discovered by the faith of His human creatures, but reveals Himself to them, thus awakening faith in their hearts. And so we Christians regard Jesus as not merely the climax of human faith in the unseen, but also, and even in a deeper and prior sense, the climax of God's revealing activity, the breaking through of the unseen into the life of humanity, the Incarnation of the Divine. And whenever we begin to lose hold of the unseen, we go back to Jesus Christ, and we say with the ancient disciple: 'No man hath seen God at any time: the only-begotten Son, who is in the bosom of the Father, he hath manifested him.'

Thus to any eager soul, wandering in the wilderness of doubt, and longing for assurance about the unseen world, there are two simple pieces of counsel that can be given. First: make sure you are following the light you have, facing the daily challenge of the unseen world, in the practical paths of duty and love. That at least must be right and must lead right. And second: remember Jesus Christ. The New Testament testifies of Him, and so does history, and so does His Church, and so do hosts of His people individually, in all sorts of conscious and unconscious ways. Do not try to find the unseen without Him. Down the whole long path of the Christian centuries, it is through Jesus Christ that people have been able to believe and trust in God.

4. THE DOCTRINE OF THE TRINITY

HARDLY any part of Christian dogma is more continually present in the worship of the Church than the doctrine of the Trinity. It is present by implication whenever a minister pronounces the threefold benediction, and more explicitly when the sacrament of baptism is administered or when the *Gloria* is said after a psalm. Yet hardly any part of Christian dogma is less present and real to the actual religious consciousness of the ordinary devout Christian. The doctrine that God consists of three persons, Father, Son and Holy Spirit, is to many people a remote and airy abstraction; they do not naturally *think* of God like that in their religious life, nor do they adjust their devotions to a Trinity, but to one God, the Father, through one Saviour and Lord, Jesus Christ: To them the word 'Trinity' suggests only a far-away mystery. Yet is it not important to find out what the doctrine really means? Is it not important to have *reality* in all our worship, and to mean something vital by the benediction and the *Gloria* and the baptismal formula, if we are going to use them at all?

What then do we *mean* by saying that God is three in one and one in three? I believe a good way of approaching that question is to ask first another question: Why do we *believe* this doctrine? Why has the Church believed it? What is it based on? Whence does it come?

I. THE BASIS OF THE DOCTRINE

Much light will be shed on the doctrine if, assuming it to be true, we can answer the question how we know it to be true. How did anybody ever discover it? How did mankind,

or how did the Church, light upon this supreme mystery—
a mystery so mysterious that it can hardly be put into words?

(1) The 'dogmatic' or rigidly scholastic answer would be
that this mystery is known to mankind simply and solely as
a matter of supernatural revelation. As is well known,
medieval and catholic orthodoxy, and also to some extent
Protestant orthodoxy, holds that, while some of the truths
of religion are accessible to reason, others could never have
been discovered unless supernaturally revealed; and further,
that while the existence of God belongs to the former class,
His threefold nature, His Trinity, belongs to the latter. That
is to say, the Christian belief in the Trinity is not due to
human reflection at all. It is not the end of a process of speculation upon the nature of things, or of a process of reflection
upon our religious experience. It is rather a *starting-point*—a
supernaturally given first principle of Christianity, which
could never have been discovered by any amount of searching, if God had not told us—but He has told us—that His
Godhead consists of three in one. Thus any traditional orthodox Confession of Faith would not put this doctrine towards
the end, as a summing-up of certain truths gradually worked
out by thought and experience (as is done in many modern
text-books), but almost at the beginning; on the ground that,
until you have laid this foundation and made clear the distinction between Father, Son and Holy Spirit, you cannot
hope to work out, or even to state, such doctrines as the
incarnation, the atonement, justification, repentance, sancti-
fication. So in our Westminster Confession, while the very
first chapter is 'of the Holy Scriptures', the second is 'of God
and of the Holy Trinity'. So also the very first of the
Thirty-nine Articles of the Church of England is 'of Faith
in the Holy Trinity'.

The result of taking the doctrine in this way as a supernaturally given dogma is that its mysteriousness seems to be

defended and excused. If a critic complains that the idea of God as three in one is unintelligible, the orthodox divine would reply that it is inevitably so. It covers a great mystery which our limited mortal minds cannot understand. We do not know what it means that there should be three Persons who are nevertheless one God. The critic may ask why we believe it if we cannot understand it—if it explains nothing but rather itself stands in need of explanation and elucidation. But the traditional divine answers that it is not as an explanation of *anything*, such as might be reached by theological thinking, that we believe it, but as a supernaturally revealed truth which must in spite of its mystery be accepted as a starting-point, which we may then try to make as reasonable as we can, shedding as much light on the mystery as is possible.

Such is the traditional attitude. Nor is it *altogether* wrong. There is some sanity in St. Anselm's famous dictum *credo ut intelligam*, and we must always be prepared in the religious realm to acknowledge a large element of mystery as the background to our little systems of belief. Moreover this doctrine of the Trinity seems *especially* to stand for the element of mystery in our apprehension of God (as we may see later). Yet that cannot be the whole truth. For no religious dogma can be simply and sheerly *given*—dictated, as it were, in definite human words in an audible voice, and taken down to be handed on in infallible Scriptures. Certainly that is not how this doctrine has come to us, for it cannot be said to be given in Scripture in any quite explicit way at all—as a doctrine of three Persons in one God. The materials for it may be given in Scripture, so that it may be a legitimate and inevitable deduction; but that is a different question. Moreover, that way of talking of the matter rests upon a wrong view of revelation, which makes *too* sharp and absolute a separation between revelation on the one hand

and reason and experience on the other. There is no such absolute gulf. God uses our minds to reveal Himself to us. Still more important, it is not ready-made dogmas that God gives us, but something much more immediate which we have to some extent to think out into doctrines. Thus it is hardly fair to say that the Trinity is so great a mystery that we cannot hope to understand it, but must just accept it; for the doctrine itself is an attempt to understand and explain and reconcile with each other certain facts and experiences of the Christian life. It may be none the less revelational in the true sense; but not as a ready-made dogma. This first view of the source and basis of the doctrine, though it has its truth to contribute, is not sufficient in itself.

(2) The next is what we may call the rationalistic or speculative view, which bases the doctrine upon a kind of natural necessity to think in a triadic way—a fundamental human conviction that ultimate reality must be of the nature of trinity in unity. There can be no doubt that apart from the historic revelation of Christianity altogether, and long before the emergence of the Christian doctrine of the Trinity, or even of the Christian religion itself, there were in various ages, and among races scattered throughout the world, tendencies to think in a threefold way about the nature of God. Turn to a book like Canon J. A. MacCulloch's *Comparative Theology*, and in the chapter on the Trinity you will find paragraphs on the appearance of this idea in the following religious traditions, which I give in their alphabetical order as they appear in the index: Babylonian, Buddhist, Egyptian, Finnish, Greek, Hindu, Jewish, Neo-Platonist, Roman, Scandinavian, Taoist. MacCulloch writes:

In the Babylonian religion we find several trinities. Thus there is the triad of the god Merodach, his consort Zarpanitu, and their son Nebo, the revealer of his father's will. These divinities were at first separate, with a worship of their own, but gradually they were drawn together, and formed a kind of family triad, which was worshipped in the city of Babylon.[1]

Something similar is found in ancient Egyptian religion, with the group of Osiris, Isis and Horus 'constituting a divine family, like the Father, Mother and Son in medieval Christian pictures.'[2] In Indian religion we have Brahma, Shiva and Vishnu. In Greek mythology we have Zeus, Hades and Poseidon, and it has been contended that these were sometimes regarded not simply as three gods, but as a trinity in unity—indeed sometimes as but three names of one and the same universal god.[3] Canon MacCulloch tells us that a clear correspondence to the Christian view is seen in the explanation given by the more mystic thinkers in ancient Rome of the division of the Capitoline Temple between Jupiter, Minerva and Juno.

> Some interpreted the three statues as signifying that Jupiter, enthroned in heaven, was the divine power; Minerva, sprung from his head, the divine wisdom; and Juno, a reduplication of Jupiter, ruling on earth.[4]

Again,

> In later Greek religion Zeus with Apollo and Athene formed a kind of triad. Athene was the reason or wisdom of Zeus, just as Apollo was the revealer of his will, which he never disregarded.[5]

To turn to Buddhism:

> Most Buddhist works begin with an invocation to Buddha, Dharma and Sangha, viz. the three Holy or Precious Ones of Buddhism; the Supreme Intelligence personified in Gautama, his law and his Church, and forming the Triratna.[6]

It is unnecessary for us to wander further round the world, but let me quote you a few sentences to sum up. Bishop Westcott wrote that 'it is impossible to study any single system of worship throughout the world without

---

[1] Op. cit., p. 88f.
[2] W. Fulton in *Encyclopaedia of Religion and Ethics*, article on 'Trinity'.
[3] MacCulloch, op. cit., p. 91.
[4] Ibid. p. 92. [5] Ibid. p. 92. [6] Ibid. p. 95.

183

being struck by the peculiar persistence of the triple number in regard to Divinity.'[1] Söderblom, so learned and sympathetic in the field of the history of religions, speaks of an apparent necessity by which all 'historical' religions cast their doctrine of God into a tri-personal form.[1]

These facts would seem to indicate that the belief in a divine Trinity, which is far older than Christianity, arose not out of any special supernatural revelation in Christ or to Christians, but out of an inherent necessity of the human mind all over the world. Indeed they seem at least to furnish proof positive that this belief did not spring *straight* from a special revelation. Yet even that is not admitted by everybody. W. E. Gladstone, for example, in his zeal for a purely revelational religion as conceived by orthodoxy, took the opposite view. Speaking of the three prongs on the trident of Poseidon in Greek mythology, he makes out that while this is indeed a symbol of the Holy Trinity, its ultimate derivation was from God's original revelation to mankind —a special revelation far back in the past in which the Trinity was supernaturally made known. This, say Gladstone and some other conservative writers, was the real source of all such traces of trinitarian thought in the pagan religions. These are to be explained, not as evolved by the human mind out of a necessity of its nature, but as degenerate relics, merging into polytheism, of an original revelation of God's triune nature.

It is hardly necessary nowadays to combat such a view. It would not explain why the doctrine is absent from the Old Testament, save at the most for some shadowy anticipations, and can hardly be said to be explicitly present in the New—though, as has been said, the materials for it are there, to be gradually worked up afterwards into the familiar doctrine. If that doctrine was indeed given in a primitive special revelation, and was corrupted by most races into

[1] See *Essays on the Trinity and the Incarnation* (ed. Rawlinson), p. 161.

polytheism, it had apparently come near to actually dying out in the religion of the very race where it ought, according to the orthodox view, to have especially survived; and that would give no explanation at all of its emergence within the Christian Church. Thus the hypothesis of an original revelation becomes *here* quite superfluous.

But what are we to say of the idea that the Christian doctrine evolved itself out of the same necessity of the human mind as produced those pagan trinities, apart from revelation of any kind? That is the view we are now considering. It is represented, for instance, by the philosopher Schlegel who says of the Trinity that 'it is the universal form of being, given by the First Cause to all His works, stamping the Seal of the Deity, if we may so speak, on all the thoughts of the mind and all the forms of nature'.[1] Usener, a learned authority on religious beginnings, speaks of a universal instinct of reverence for the number three among primitive peoples; while Leisegang, another investigator in this field, attributes the emergence of the idea to 'a compulsion arising out of the exigencies of mystical experience'.[2] Even Aristotle wrote that 'all things are three, and three is everywhere, since, as the Pythogoreans say, the all and all things are determined by the number three'[3]; and we might quote also from such thinkers as Philo Judaeus and Plotinus. Moreover, we must remember that St. Augustine himself worked out a philosophical doctrine of the Trinity, based on the argument that since God eternally is love, He must from all eternity have had an object of love within His Godhead, and that, if there is thus a Lover and a Loved, there must needs also be a Relation between them as eternal as themselves. Thus, while the Father eternally

---

[1] MacCulloch, *op. cit.*, p. 88.

[2] These references to Usener and Leisegang are made by Kenneth Kirk in *Essays on the Trinity and the Incarnation* (ed. Rawlinson), p. 161ff.

[3] *De Caelo*, 11; quoted by Kirk, *op. cit.*, p. 175n.

loves the Son, 'the Holy Spirit is the communion of Godhead, the mutual affection and love of the Father and the Son'.[1]

The climax of all this kind of thing may be said to be found in the Hegelian doctrine. The whole of Hegel's philosophy is based on the notion that all reality and all knowledge are threefold in pattern or movement. There are the thesis, the antithesis, and then the synthesis which comprehends and reconciles the other two. This notion of a triadic synthesis has been applied to our doctrine by saying that the Absolute comprehends 'being in itself', 'being for itself' and 'being in and for itself'.

Now all these constructions might be taken as lending support to the view that the doctrine of the Trinity is a natural and necessary expression of the essential nature of reality, and so it might be argued that it was this tendency, already widespread in the world, that led the Christian Church gradually to adopt the view that God is three in one, and one in three. It was not thus a revealed truth, but rather a necessity of thought, recognised by many races, and so prevalently expressed in the times when Christian dogma was being formed that the Church was inevitably driven along the same path.

What are we to say to this view. We need not hesitate to acknowledge that there may be *some* truth in it. No doubt the number three *has* been very widely regarded as somehow the perfect number—or as a sacred, symbolic or divine number; and the fact that it plays such an important part both in Christianity and in the ethnic religions can hardly be quite accidental. No doubt it is true also that the Christian adoption of the trinitarian view was *prepared* for by all these pagan notions. The minds of many people must thus have been ready for the belief that God was three in one. That

[1] *De Fid. et Symbol.*, 9.

need not disconcert us. I do not see why we should ever be disconcerted by discovering that ideas which we believed to have been given by Christian revelation were anticipated by, or can be paralleled by, the mythologies of paganism. It only indicates how well fitted are the Christian ideas to the human mind. After all, if these ideas are true and right, should we not expect to find some gleams of that eternal divine truth reaching the groping, blundering minds of the pagan races, at least in the form of a promise or a need which Christianity would afterwards meet and fulfil?

Moreover, does it not seem likely that one of the factors leading to the development of this Christian doctrine was the half-conscious desire to have a richer, warmer idea of deity than a bare and cold monotheism could provide? That certainly was one of the motives leading to the formation within Hebrew thought of such ideas as the personified Word or Wisdom of God. The One God was so remote that people were impelled to believe in an intermediary Wisdom or Logos, such as might unite God to man. And may not the same be true of the further step—towards a Trinity—taken in Christian theology? Men could not be satisfied with thinking of God as a starkly solitary Person, existing above from all eternity until the creation of finite beings. Such a God could hardly even be thought of as love; and so a richer idea had to be reached. Some would say that even in pre-Christian Judaism, within the Old Testament, this tendency went so far as to produce a kind of Trinity—of God, His Wisdom or Word, and His Spirit. And there is some truth in the view that Christianity inherited this tendency, and by the same kind of intellectual necessity arrived at its own doctrine.

There is thus *some* truth in the 'speculative' view. But we must now go on to point out how inadequate is that view when taken by itself.

(a) For one thing, the parallels between ethnic trinities and the Christian conception are not nearly so real as might be supposed. In fact it might be said that many or most of the pagan examples do not exhibit trinity in unity at all. These were not really cases of three Persons in One God, but rather of three gods; so that what we have is not a trinity, still less a triunity, but a tritheism. If Christianity developed its doctrine of the Trinity out of a high and severe mono-theism, so as to save that monotheism from becoming *too* stark and solitary, the pagan religions developed their trinity rather as *an inset into a gross and luxuriant polytheism.* There is a very great difference here.

(b) For another thing, it cannot really be maintained that the prevailing tendency in the Jewish and pagan environment of early Christianity was towards a trinitarian conception. Bishop Kenneth Kirk, who went very carefully into this matter, maintained that there was in the air much more of a *binitarian* than of a trinitarian tendency. Religion might think of God and a Logos—the one supreme God and an intermediary between Him and man. Even Judaism, with its God, its Wisdom of God, and its Word of God, did not really present a trinitarian idea. It did not think of the Wis-dom and the Word as quite distinct *hypostases.* These were certainly personified in a sense, but the Jews thought of them rather as *personifications* than as persons; they could merge into each other; or perhaps were rather but different names for the same reality, the one used in one school and the other in another. Thus nobody would speak in a symmetrical triad of God and His Wisdom and His Word, but some would speak of God and His Word, others of God and His Wisdom. The same is perhaps true even when we come to consider the conception of the Spirit of God in Judaism. Did people really make a distinction between the Word and the Spirit in any fixed way? Was it not rather that in some environments people would speak of God as acting on us 'through His Word', and in other environments they would say 'through His Spirit'? Thus, so far as the idea was fixed at all, it was a *binitarian* idea; on the one hand, the one great God over all; on the other, His Spirit or Word or Wisdom, as His medium in communicating with His world, or even in creating it. Thus the environment and inheritance of early Christianity made rather for a binitarian than a trinitarian formulation. Kirk shows how this even persisted into the thought of Christianity itself, in the New Testament and later[1]; and goes on to make the point that it was not through being moulded by an already prevailing trinitarian tendency that Christianity was led to its own doctrine, but rather through a long struggle against an existing binitarian tendency, being impelled by an inward necessity of its own. It seems at least safe to say that the prevalence of a trinitarian idea of the Godhead in that age has been greatly exaggerated.

(c) Further, if we consider the idea that there is in the human mind an inherent necessity to see ultimate reality in a threefold way, it is only to realise that that truth also is capable of being greatly exaggerated. It cannot after all be said to be a very fundamental thought in most of the philosophers instanced above—though perhaps it was for the Pythagoreans and in another way for the Hegelians. No doubt three has often been looked upon as the perfect number. But so have other numbers: sometimes the number four (to be four-square means to be complete); or the number five (the fingers of one hand); or the number seven (indeed seven most of all, as you can see from different parts of the Bible); or the number twelve (as you can see in the Bible also). That kind of thing takes you no distance at all

---

[1] Cf. the idea of Christ as a *deuteros theos*, while there was no word of a *tritos theos*. Origen uses this phrase of the Logos, as Philo had done before him.

towards understanding the emergence of the Christian doctrine of the Trinity.

It is indeed perfectly true that Christianity did not invent or discover the doctrine, or receive it by revelation, as a completely new and original truth; no, there had been adumbrations of it in almost world-wide speculation. But that in itself does not explain it. Nothing that we have hitherto said is enough to explain it. Nothing can do that until we come to certain definite Christian facts and experiences.

(3) We thus come, in the third place, to the view that it was based on Christian history and experience—neither on special revelation in the narrow sense nor on general speculation in the wide sense, but on historic facts and experiences which had to be interpreted by the Christian Church. This is the mode of approach which I now wish to follow. Not that even this approach, taken narrowly by itself, is quite satisfactory; for so much is implied in our admission that there is some truth in the other approaches. But the central truth is with the third view, which I must now try to expound.

II. The Historic Facts

The primary fact which gave rise to this whole movement of theological thought was the historical fact of Jesus. The career of Jesus on earth was so stupendous a fact—His person, His teaching, His works, His power, His cross, His victory— that His followers were faced with an urgent task of explanation. He had made everything different for them, had brought God into their lives in a wholly new way—and forgiveness and joy and power and victory over sin and care and death. And though He was Himself put to death, that was not defeat, for they knew that that very death had won for them the greatest thing of all, that somehow it was an atoning death in which God had reconciled sinners to Himself. But how could this be? Only one explanation could suffice: that *God was in Christ*. All that Jesus was and did and suffered—it was not simply Jesus. Somehow it was God. God was in it, sharing in it all, even in the sacrifice. But how? Was Jesus simply identical with God? Is 'Jesus' just another name for God? No, that could not be the truth; for Jesus was a man—quite genuinely a man; not only in body but in mind. He spoke about God and prayed to Him, so He must have been distinct from God. Moreover, He was subject to the limitations of humanity: He was not omniscient, He was not raised clear above the struggle with temptation, He suffered and He died. But none of these things could be said of God *simpliciter*. God did not die upon the Cross; it was only heretics, the Patripassians, who said He did, and their heresy on this point showed precisely that they had an inadequate view of the Trinity, the Sabellian view, as we shall see later. Yet if Jesus was not simply God dwelling in a human body, what was He? Was He another God, alongside of the Father, or some sort of semi-divine being, half God and half man? No, that would not do either. For to think of Him thus would be a clear departure from monotheism, and while a too bare monotheism may need to be corrected and enriched, Christianity could never agree to depart from essential monotheism even by a hairsbreadth, or to take the shortest step towards anything like polytheism. On the other hand, if instead of calling Christ a second God, you make Him a semi-divine being, subordinate to the Father and quite distinct from Him, then you leave the Father out of the whole business of redemption—you have no real incarnation of God at all, nor any divine atonement for human sin. That is where the Arians went astray; not in making Jesus a mere man, for they certainly never did that, and indeed it would be truer to say that they denied the manhood of Christ altogether; but they made Him a kind of demigod distinct from the Father; and the Church could never tolerate that, partly because it savoured of polytheism, and partly because it yielded no sort of assurance about God Himself and His attitude to sinners.

Thus the Church was driven to make a much finer distinction. It was driven to the conviction that while Jesus was not identical with God, God was incarnate in Him. Yet not wholly or absolutely so, but in respect of one *hypostasis* or *persona* of God. There could be only one God; but God existed in more than one *hypostasis* or *persona*, one of which became incarnate in Jesus Christ, uniting with human nature in Him.

But what further could be said in order to distinguish this *hypostasis* from the others? Sometimes the Church tried to distinguish it by saying it was the Logos or Word of God. This would convey something to both Jews and Gentiles, since the Old Testament had spoken much of the Word of God, and so had Philo, while the Greeks (Platonists and others) had spoken of the Logos, one of whose meanings in Greek is 'word'. But there was another expression which was more akin to Jesus' own way of talking and thinking. He continually spoke of God as the Father, and had Himself a very living sense of *Sonship*. The Church could never get away from that, and so they inevitably spoke of the second *hypostasis* as the Son. There was God the Father and there was God the Son, and yet not two Gods but one. We shall speak later of the meaning of the term *hypostasis* or *persona*, but meanwhile we are trying to see the historic facts and experiences out of which it arose. And the first of these is the disciples' experience of the fact of Jesus.

There is, however, another fact and experience which went to the making of the doctrine of the Trinity, and we may conveniently and briefly indicate it by the one word *Pentecost*. Let us begin by remembering that the disciples had their Master with them in the flesh for only a few brief years, and that no other Christians since then have had that experience at all. To the disciples it was indeed a very marvellous experience, the very light of life. When Jesus was by their side, God was real to them as He had never been before. They depended upon Him in everything. And if they ever saw clearly that their Master was going to be suddenly taken from them by a violent and shameful death, the prospect was too terrible to be faced. How could they ever get along without Him? Their religion would collapse utterly, and God would fade out of their lives! Well, the blow did fall, and Jesus was crucified as a criminal. And yet, if a few months later you had asked these same disciples how it had fared with their faith, and whether they had now altogether lost God out of their lives, they would have replied with a very joyful and unanimous 'No'. In fact they would have told you that somehow the presence of God was now far more real and wonderful and powerful than it had been even when Jesus was with them in the flesh. Perhaps their faith did suffer a temporary collapse at the Crucifixion, but that was very temporary indeed. It soon burned up more strongly than ever. I am not going to speak in this place of their resurrection-experiences two or three days after the Crucifixion, though these had of course a great deal to do with the revival of their faith, because for our present purpose there is another experience which is even more directly relevant. It was about seven weeks after their Master's death; and on the day of the Jewish feast called Pentecost. The disciples and some others who had become Christians were assembled for fellowship and worship in a certain room, when there came upon them an overpowering sense of the presence and power of God—the God whom they had learned to know through Jesus. This was something far more wonderful even than what had been theirs when their Master was with them in the flesh. They felt now that, instead of having lost God when Jesus was taken from them, they had lost neither Jesus nor God. Jesus seemed nearer than ever, and God had come into their lives as never before, so that they could go out and bear witness for Him.

I wonder if an analogy might help us to understand it, though it can be but a faint and inadequate analogy. Let us imagine a young fellow who owes a very great deal, religiously, to his father. His father has been to him almost a revelation of God. While his father's fine, strong, devout personality is beside him, God is real to him, so that he comes to have a lively, eager faith of his own, though very much in dependence upon his father. Then the father is stricken down by illness which moves to a fatal conclusion; and as the young man sees the end approaching, he feels as if it would be the end of all things for him, or at least for his faith. If his father is taken from him, he will never be able to find God for himself again. Well, the end does come. His father dies. Perhaps for a very brief space the youth is so stricken in spirit that God seems unreal. But that does not last long. The sense of God's presence comes back—and is stronger than ever. The unseen world, into which his father has passed, seems nearer and more real than before. He himself comes to have a firmer hold on God than before, because now that he can no longer rely on his father's bodily presence, he is thrown back directly upon the eternal God Himself. And this is the best thing that could possibly have happened to his faith. Though it seemed so terrible in advance, yet it was *expedient* for him.

Can that be taken as a faint analogy of the experience of the disciples? They found that somehow Jesus, hidden from their eyes in the unseen world, could do more for them than ever, and that, contrary to all their fears, God's presence was a more powerful thing to them now than even in the days when their Master was with them in the flesh. Does that not help us to understand the significance of the words in the Fourth Gospel about His approaching death?

> But because I have said these things unto you, sorrow hath filled your heart. Nevertheless I tell you the truth; It is expedient for you that I go away: for if I go not away, the Comforter will not come unto you; but if I depart, I will send him unto you.[1]

After He departed, the Presence became more marvellous than ever—and more *universal*. It was a more timeless, space-less thing to them now; they could enjoy it wherever they went, in society or in solitude. Of course they owed it all to what Jesus had done for them, but they now found that it need not be confined to those who had known Him in the flesh. This was a thing that anybody could have anywhere. To tell men the story of Jesus was enough, and then time after time the wonderful thing would happen, and the Presence would come into their lives. Wherever they carried the story of Jesus, it went on happening, just as it had happened to the disciples themselves on the day of Pentecost.

It was a *fact of experience*. But now, when those early Christians set out to describe and explain it, what were they to say about it? What was this wonderful new Presence? Was it simply the Jesus they had known, come back to them 'unseen but not unknown'? No, that was not quite the right description. They did indeed sometimes speak of it as the presence of Christ with them or in them. That *was* one way of speaking of it. Yet it was not quite the same; it was something really greater and more universal; the same experience, and yet different; the same, yet deepened and widened, freed from all limitations of space and time. Was it then the very presence of God Himself? Yes; but some further definition of it was required. This was something new in their knowledge of God. This was something in

[1] John 6.6-7.

God which they had not known before. How were they to describe or define it?

Well, they could not but remember that in the Old Testament, when such a Presence and power came now and again upon certain exceptional men here and there, it was described as the *Spirit* of God coming upon them—poured out upon them. This Spirit was not different from God Himself, not separate from Him; yet the phrase seemed to be required to describe the experience of these exceptional men. But then it was remembered also that in the Old Testament the prophet Joel had foretold that the time would come when God would pour out His Spirit, not on exceptional people only, but on all sorts of ordinary people, even servants and handmaidens.[1] Further, it would be remembered that Jesus Himself had also spoken of God giving His Holy Spirit to all who really asked for this gift, and had promised His disciples that, when they were in straits, the Spirit of God would guide them, and teach them what to say.[2] Many other things had He said to them about their receiving the gift of the Spirit in their need—though we cannot be sure how far St. John 14-16 represents His *ipsissima verba*. Hence, when they looked back afterwards, having already experienced that wonderful Presence and power, and asked themselves what it was and what it meant, they said not just 'This is God', not just 'This is Jesus', but 'This is God's Spirit'. This, they said, is what Joel predicted would one day happen—so St. Peter is reported to have put it on the day of Pentecost. It is what Jesus promised. It is the gift of the Holy Spirit. Throughout the New Testament it is a mark of Christians that they not only believed in Christ and followed Him, but also had something of that experience which is described as receiving the Holy Spirit.

[1] Joel 2.28ff.
[2] Luke 11.13; Matthew 10.19f; Luke 12.12.

To sum up, then: if these are the historic facts, it emerges that the early Christians, in endeavouring to define or explain their Christian experiences, had three centres or foci of experience to reckon with—not two, but three. St. Paul, in giving his blessing at the end of a letter, would write: 'The grace of the Lord Jesus Christ, and the love of God, and the communion of the Holy Spirit be with you all.' The historic facts and experiences led him to speak in that way. The New Testament does not carry us much further than that, but we may compare the baptismal formula in St. Matthew[2] (though this was not the earliest formula, in which baptism was into or in the name of Christ). As has been said, the New Testament does not provide a finished doctrine of the Trinity, but only the materials for it. But when afterwards the Church was led to distinguish different Persons (*hypostases* or *personae*) in the Godhead, they had to distinguish not two but three; and not three Gods, for there was only one God; but in the one substance (*ousia* or *substantia*) of the Godhead three Persons. This came to be the orthodox statement, and I have tried to show how naturally it grew out of the historic facts and experiences.

III. THE MEANING OF THE DOCTRINE

It is of the highest importance to consider carefully the terms employed in this orthodox statement. Much confusion and perplexity is caused by forgetting that the word 'person' does not here mean precisely what we mean by 'person' or 'personality' nowadays. It is sometimes assumed that the terms used were quite simple and unambiguous; one substance but three Persons, one *ousia* or *substantia* but three *hypostaseis* or *personae*. But in fact there was a great deal of variation, and of groping, before just these terms came to be adopted by the Church—as well as much variation and

[1] Chapter 28.19

uncertainty about the meaning of the terms themselves. The Greek *ousia* is the term which came to be represented in Latin by *substantia*, though structurally and etymologically that latter would rather correspond to the Greek *hypostasis*. As a matter of fact, these two Greek words, *ousia* and *hypostasis*, which later had to be distinguished sharply, seem at first to have meant the same thing and to be used interchangeably. Though the orthodox position later came to be that Christ was of one *ousia* with the Father, but was a different *hypostasis*, yet the Nicene Creed pronounced anathema on those who say that the Son is of another *hypostasis* or *ousia* than the Father—the two terms being here used interchangeably. Thus the Nicene Creed anathematised, as far as words are concerned, what afterwards became orthodox. It has also been pointed out that Origen used the two words interchangeably; and as late as A.D. 450 we find Theodoret asking what is the difference between them and replying: 'According to the secular philosopher there is no difference, since *ousia* signifies being, and *hypostasis* signifies an existence.' Eventually, however, a Christian distinction did develop.

According to some authorities this was brought about through the compromise proposed *after* the Nicene Council for the reconciliation of the two parties. The decision of the Council itself was somewhat forced. The parties were not so diametrically opposed as was made to appear. The Arians, with the exception of the extremists, ultimately gave up the three *ousiai* and agreed that there was only one *ousia* in the Godhead, while for the distinctions within the Godhead the term *hypostasis* came to be used. It seems to have been the Cappadocian Fathers—the two Gregories and St. Basil in the latter half of the fourth century—who definitely appropriated these Greek words for what became the orthodox usage in the formula 'one *ousia* and three *hypostaseis*'; though there are traces of that formula nearly a century earlier in Alexandria.[1] But this development was largely conditioned by the fact that by this time the Latin Fathers had chosen *persona* as their word for expressing the distinctions within the Godhead.

It seems to be Tertullian, a lawyer, who first employed this term. What did he mean by it? Originally, in classical Latin, it meant the mask worn by an actor, and hence also an actor's *part* in any particular play. From this it came to mean, in legal terminology, a party to a transaction or dispute; not simply an individual person as such, but rather as involved in a certain relationship and playing a certain part within that relationship; but there was as yet no suggestion of what we might call the philosophical use of the word, as connoting a self-conscious moral personality. This then was the word selected by Tertullian to express distinctions in the Godhead. By employing it he intended to steer clear of tritheism on the one hand, and on the other hand of a Sabellianism which would altogether remove the substantive distinction between Father, Son and Holy Spirit. Harnack's suggestion is that to the lawyer Tertullian the word *substantia* meant property in the legal sense, and that he was thinking of how three legal parties (*personae*) can be united in jointly holding one property; but this seems too crudely legal even for Tertullian. At all events, the latter did not think of the three persons as personalities in the modern sense. That is plain from the figures he uses:

> God brought forth the Word (even as the Paraclete also teaches) as the root does the shrub, the source the river, and the sun the ray. For these forms too are projections of the natures from which they proceed. Nor should I hesitate to call the Son both the shrub of the root and the river of the source and the ray of the sun, because every origin is a parent, and all that is brought forth from the origin is offspring, much more the Word of God, which also in a real sense

[1] Cf. F. W. Green in *Essays on the Trinity and the Incarnation* (ed. Rawlinson) pp. 247ff.

o

received the name of Son. And yet the shrub is not distinguished from the root, nor the river from the source, nor the ray from the sun, even as the Word is not distinguished from God either. . . . The Spirit is third with respect to God and the Son, even as the fruit from the shrub is third from the root, and the channel from the river is third from the source, and the point where the ray strikes something is third from the sun. Yet in no respect is it banished from the original source from which it derives its special qualities. Thus the Trinity running down from the Father through stages linked and united together, offers no obstacle to monarchy and conserves the established position of the economy.[1]

Tertullian certainly cannot be suspected of minimising the distinction between the persons in the Godhead, for it was against the 'Sabellianising' Praxeas that he wrote the treatise from which I take these words. But the images here used, and indeed the passage as a whole, make it clear that he did not think of the three Persons as three separate 'personalities', three several minds or centres of consciousness, in the modern sense.

Now, when the Latin word *persona* came to be put into Greek, the most obvious rendering would have been *prosopon*, which meant originally face or countenance, but which had come to carry the same secondary meaning as *persona*—aspect, mask, person. But the Greek theologians on the whole fought shy of this word as a trinitarian term, perhaps as savouring too much of the Sabellianising tendency to make the three Persons no more than three successive aspects, or three successive parts played. So the word preferred was rather *hypostasis*. There was no special reason, whether of meaning or of etymology, why this should be regarded as a suitable translation. *Hypostasis* means an actual, concrete, individual bit of reality, as contrasted with a mere abstraction, such as an aspect or quality which has no hypostatic existence of its own. No doubt, therefore, the word was chosen to indicate that the distinctions within the Godhead were real,

[1] *Adversus Praxean*, 8; Souter's translation in *Tertullian Against Praxeas*, p. 44f.

inherent, substantive, and not merely abstract or adjectival. Some other Greek word might have been chosen, just as some Latin word other than *persona* might have been chosen; but, once chosen, the words doubtless affected each other in meaning and usage, and they both came to be the accepted terms. They were never given any kind of impersonal meaning; for nothing in God is impersonal. That is vital, and the Church could not be tempted away from it. But on the other hand the Church could not be persuaded into any kind of tritheism—though there *was* a temptation in this direction, and some ancient divines came very near to succumbing. So the Church did not mean that the three Persons of the Trinity were as distinct from each other as three separate persons, personalities or minds as we use these terms today. The three Persons were *one* God.

In the early fathers from St. Athanasius onwards there are various signs of the attempt to safeguard this truth by insisting on the inseparability of the Persons. In St. Athanasius there is the beginning of the use of the Greek word *perichoresis* to indicate that the Father and the Son *interpenetrate* each other. The word was used also by Gregory of Nissa to mean that the Persons do not act separately but conjointly. A corresponding Latin term, *circumincessio* is found in St. Hilary of Poitiers, expressing the idea that the three Persons interpenetrate by their mutual love for one another.[1] We may note also that the Cappadocian Fathers, though they are generally regarded as going further than the main stream of thought in the direction of conceiving three distinct personalities, nevertheless used the phrase 'modes of being' as well as *hypostasis* and taught that the whole of God is in each of the three Persons.

Still more important is St. Augustine's way of speaking of the doctrine. He offers several different images for its

---

[1] Cf. John 17.21-25.

illumination. It was he who first broached the idea that, if God is eternally Love, He must from all eternity, and hence since before creation, have an object of Love within the Godhead, and that in such a case there must also be a third entity—the relation of Love between the Lover and the Loved. 'The Holy Spirit is the communion of Godhead, the mutual affection and love between the Father and the Son.'[1] In another place he says that the Son is Wisdom, and the Spirit is Love. Elsewhere again, he finds an analogy of the Trinity in the constitution of the human mind, in which there are reflection and love, which are yet of one substance with mind. Once more, human personality consists of memory, intelligence and will, and these are three in one. Finally, in perception there are the object seen, the vision, and the attention of the observer. He uses all these analogies from the human soul, because, being the image of God, it reflects His three-in-oneness. All of which surely indicates that the great African thinker did not conceive of the three Persons as separate personalities. Remember his famous saying: 'We say three Persons, not in order that such a statement may be made, but in order to avoid saying nothing.'[2] So strong was his sense that all our utterances concerning this doctrine are inadequate human attempts to express what is really beyond our comprehension.

In the light of all this it will be well for us to beware of making a more hard and fast distinction or separation between the Persons than was intended by the Church in its declarations or by the great theologians in their explanations. St. Bernard said: 'Let us not admit multiplicity into the Trinity, nor solitude into its unity.' Sometimes the attempt has been made to base the doctrine on experience in a somewhat artificial way, tracing the different parts of our religious experience to the three Persons respectively; as if we could

[1] *De Fid. et Symbol.*, 9.   [2] *De Trinitate*, 5, 14.

say definitely, for instance, that when as creatures we are conscious of the almighty Creator and praise and worship Him, that is an experience of the Father; when we are conscious of warm and intimate divine companionship, that is experience of the Son; and when we are conscious of an overpowering divine influence, such as lifts us above ourselves without or against our own wills, that is an experience of the Holy Spirit. No doubt there is some truth in this. But not when put in this cut-and-dried way, the rigidity of which is as foreign to our actual experience as it is to Scripture and to the great early theologians. Surely we are not entitled to say that part of our life as Christians derives from the Father alone, part from the Son, and part from the Spirit, as if there were no *perichoresis* or *circumincessio*. It is an old principle: *opera trinitatis ad extra sunt indivisa*. The New Testament tells us that no one can come to the Father except through the Son; that no one can come to the Son unless the Father draws him; that it is the Father who gives us the Holy Spirit, who will take of the things of Christ and show them to us; and that it is through the Spirit that Christ dwells with His people. Take those great chapters of the Fourth Gospel, fourteen to sixteen, where we find so much about the Father, about the presence and comfort of Christ, and about the work of the Paraclete. They may be taken as answering the question, sure to be asked by the second and third generation, how the Christians of that later age could make up for the lack of what the first disciples had enjoyed— actual intercourse with Jesus on earth. Could anything make up for it? Could an old, old story, however wonderful, avail so much to those who had not *seen*? Nor can we, after nineteen centuries, sometimes help asking the same question. But the answer given in these chapters is that there is a living spiritual Presence which can do even more for us than the earthly life of Jesus could do; a Presence that has not ceased and never will cease. When we ask what it is, whether the eternal God Himself, or the continued Presence of Jesus, or the Holy Spirit now given to us, these great chapters seem to mingle all three ways of putting it inextricably and interchangeably, as if there were not three different realities, but three ways of expressing the same experience.

For in some verses it is Jesus Himself who is going to come and be with His disciples all their days. In others it is the Holy Spirit, whom He is going to *send*. In still others it seems to be the eternal Father that the disciples have to depend on now. But all three ideas are strangely intermingled.[1] Yet is that altogether strange? Do Christian readers find it strange? Does it not remind them that if they speak of the Presence as the Living Christ (as they will continue to do), they must not allow that either to blind them to the idea of the Living God or, worse still, to suggest that there is in the background a God less gracious and accessible than Jesus Christ; or again, in another direction, to obscure the features of the historical Jesus. Jesus is not a substitute for God, nor is He simply identical with God the Father, nor is He the second God, nor is the Holy Spirit a third God. God is one and eternal, and Jesus was a definite historical figure in time. Yet it was God Himself who was incarnate in Jesus, who still comes to us through Jesus—who also leads us to Jesus and reveals Him to us. With all its difficulties and obscurities the doctrine of the Trinity has enabled the Church to hold and to express that truth while avoiding the errors that so easily beset us on every side.

It may be worth while to bring all this to a conclusion by mentioning again, in the light of what has now been said, the actual dangers which the doctrine was meant to avert, as we see them raising their heads in the great heresies.

[1] Read, for example, such verses as John 14.16-20; John 16.26ff; John 14.25, 26, 28; John 15.26ff; John 17.20.

(1) On the one hand, there was the danger of making too sharp a distinction between the Divine which was manifest in Jesus and the eternal Father Himself. The result of that would be either a relapse into polytheism or a loss of the reality of the incarnation. That was the danger of the Arian movement, the Arians really falling into both errors. They made the Logos a sort of demigod alongside of the Father, which was a concession to polytheism; and then, since it was only this demigod and not the eternal God Himself who became incarnate in Jesus, there was no real *divine* incarnation at all, and we were left without any real assurance as to how the eternal God Himself was disposed towards us. No wonder that Athanasius opposed this error, or that the Church rejected it.

(2) But on the other hand there was the danger of ignoring altogether the distinction within the divine nature between the eternal Father and the divine Logos. This was the danger of falling back into a stark and remote monotheism that was too simple for the facts, and it appeared in two quite different forms.

It appeared in the Ebionite and Adoptionist form—that very early class of heresies, springing mainly from a conservative Jewish Christianity, which would not be moved away from the starkest Jewish monotheism, and therefore could say no more about Jesus than that He was a man who attained such goodness and spiritual power that He was raised by God to messianic and heavenly dignity. Here again we have no real incarnation of God at all, but at the most a deification of man—though even deification would be too strong a word, since it is rather a case of *adoption*.

But the same danger appeared in the very different direction of Modalistic Monarchianism—the type of view which reduced all distinctions within the divine nature to mere differences of *mode* or *aspect*; thus maintaining a very monarchical view of Deity, a very strict unity, but at the same time doing what the Ebionites and Adoptionists did not do —maintaining a very exalted view of the nature of Christ as divine and safeguarding the reality of the incarnation. This tendency appeared about the end of the second century, being represented in Praxeas, Noëtus and Sabellius. Obviously it resulted in a different kind of error; since if there is no distinction between the first and second Persons of the Trinity, between Christ and God, then it was God the Father Himself who suffered and died on the Cross—and this was the Patripassian heresy. The Church could not tolerate this; and I may remind you of the brilliant but bitter remark made by Tertullian about Praxeas. Holding the Modalist view, and thus hardly able to avoid Patripassianism, Praxeas might seem to have left no room at all for the Holy Spirit. Moreover he was strongly opposed to the Montanists who made so much of the doctrine of the Spirit, and Tertullian was a Montanist. 'Praxeas,' said Tertullian, 'did two jobs for the Devil at Rome. He drove out prophecy and he brought in heresy; he put to flight the Paraclete and he crucified the Father'.[1] Not that this was fair to Praxeas or the Sabellians, but it does point out one dangerous tendency.

It was, then, to avoid these various heresies, tending in two opposite directions, that the doctrine of the Trinity came to be gradually worked out; and however difficult the distinctions it makes may sometimes seem to us, they do stand at every point for some vital concern of our faith. It was fundamental to maintain that God was incarnate in Jesus. Yet not altogether or *simpliciter*. Else how could Jesus pray *to* God as He did? Or who was ruling the universe during the years that God was incarnate in one particular and limited human life in Palestine? And did God die on the Cross? *But,* if God was not altogether incarnate in Jesus, could it then be

[1] *Adversus Praxean*, I.

said that *part* of Him was? No, that way of putting it could not be right, for God is 'without parts'[1]; and in any case, if it were just one part of God among others that was incarnate, we should have thereby no sure guarantee as to what other parts of Him would be like, or how they might be disposed towards us. Hence the Church felt that, whatever distinction had to be made, it must be maintained that somehow the whole fulness of God dwelt in Jesus. Can we then say, instead of one part, one *aspect* of God—that the whole God-head revealed one aspect of Himself in the incarnation, or that He revealed the whole of His being under one aspect? That seems nearer the truth. Yet the word *aspect* suggests something purely relative to the human mind, so that there might be any number of aspects varying with our point of view. Or even if the aspects are limited to three, the word suggests something shifting and transitory; and Sabellius did indeed regard the three Persons as *successive* manifestations of God—the Father in the Old Testament, the Son in the incarnation, and the Spirit in the continued life of the Church. And why could the Church not be content with that? The Latin word *persona* might indeed suggest something of this sort—an actor's mask or an actor's part; but it is significant that when a Greek equivalent had to be found, the naturally corresponding word (*prosopon*) was avoided, because it even more definitely carried the false suggestion of a merely passing aspect, a merely relative distinction. They must find a word that would express a *substantive* distinction; a word which would neither imperil the divine unity, dividing God into parts, nor suggest that He played merely successive rôles. They must come to rest in between these two errors. So, retaining the word *persona* in Latin, they fixed on the word *hypostasis* in Greek. Neither word was quite unambigu-

---

[1] As in the Westminster Confession, Chapter II, and the first of the Thirty-nine Articles.

ous or above suspicion. But their dangers lay in opposite directions. Used unintelligently, either word can lead men's minds away from the truth; and that has sometimes happened.

Moreover, we must remember that in nearly all cases of heresy there is *something* to be said on the side of the heretics, their error being partly due to the Church's use of ambiguous terms which could so easily be misunderstood. Hence we must always be on our guard against using the orthodox formulas too mechanically, without stopping to ask what we mean by them. Subject, however, to these safeguards and explanations the Church holds that the Godhead consists of one *ousia* or *substantia*, and three *hypostaseis* or *personae*.

.   .   .   .   .   .

All these explanations having been made, however, I feel that some of you may still be asking whether I have really offered anything more than an *historical* justification of the doctrine of the Holy Trinity, and whether it is really a natural or necessary expression of our Christian faith today. And where some have especial difficulty is with relation to the third Person—the Holy Spirit. We can see, they say, that God and Christ must come into any creed—God the Father almighty and God incarnate in Christ. These are inevitable foci of all our thought of God and all our worship of Him. But why a third focus? Why the Holy Spirit?

Much of the answer to this challenge was contained in what I have already said, when I tried to show how the doctrine arose out of history and experience, and then went on to trace the specific historic facts giving rise to it—the fact of Jesus and the fact of Pentecost. But perhaps I can do a little more to show how these two facts added something to the thought of God, so that the monotheism inherited from Israel and the Old Testament had inevitably to grow into something richer without becoming one whit less monotheistic.

It is hardly necessary to say more about the distinction between the Father and the Son. The figure of Jesus undoubtedly brought something new into the knowledge of God, even among those who had inherited Israel's faith. Here was God appearing in a human life on earth. Here was God dwelling in man in a way for which there had hitherto been no vocabulary. Or if there were certain suggestions of a ready-made vocabulary in such terms as the Logos or Word, yet these had to be used now in a new way. Thus it was inevitable that Christians should come to distinguish between God the Father and God the Word or Son. That is plain sailing.

But why a third term? Why the Holy Spirit? It is because, while our Christian experience of God is different from anything that existed before Christ came, yet on the one hand it is not identical with Christ's own experience of God but is rather dependent upon that perfect experience, while on the other hand it is not identical with the experience of the disciples during Christ's earthly life, since we have not seen Him in the flesh and never can. Yet we are not really at any disadvantage as compared with them, since our Christian knowledge of God is of a kind which was not possible before the Incarnation but is now available to anybody in any age. This is what makes the third term necessary. This is why the monotheism inherited from Israel had to develop into the threefold affirmation.

Needless to say, this does not mean that God had changed since the days when He revealed Himself to Israel—as if God the Son had come into existence at a later date, and the Spirit at a later date still. No, Christianity has always taught that the Son existed from all eternity, co-eternal with the Father; and the same is true of the Holy Spirit. St. Paul himself says that the Spiritual Rock which followed the Israelites through the wilderness in the days of Moses was Christ. Nor was the

Spirit which came at Pentecost something new in God, but the very Spirit so much spoken of in the Old Testament. The new thing was that God became incarnate, and that as a result there came a wonderful new experience of Him which could be described only as an outpouring of His Spirit. It was of course the one Triune God who revealed Himself to the patriarchs and the prophets, but in Jesus Christ He revealed Himself more fully, and it was the reception of this fuller revelation that resulted in a doctrine which retained the old monotheism but developed it into the richer conception of the Triune. I have said repeatedly that we have not here to do with three separate personalities in the modern sense of that word, and this may lead you to ask me, 'Do you not then believe in the personality of the Holy Spirit? Is He not then personal?' My answer is, 'Yes, certainly I do, because the Spirit is God, and God is personal. God is wholly personal, and there is nothing impersonal in His being, or in any of His activities.' We must never speak or think about God in an impersonal way. Yet the doctrine of the three Persons does not mean that these represent three parts of God, and that each of them is a separate personality. Catholic theology, as I have said, has always taught that God has no parts, and that the whole fulness of God is in each of the three Persons. That is why Karl Barth prefers to speak of 'modes of being' rather than 'persons'. Yet this is not a heretical 'Modalism', so long as we do not think of temporally successive modes, or merely of three aspects arbitrarily and subjectively selected out of a possible indefinite number, with an 'essence' of God lying behind them and different from them all. . . .[1]

I fear you may have found this long treatment of the doctrine of the Trinity somewhat confusing. That is perhaps

[1] Here is omitted a somewhat full consideration of the *filioque* clause in the Nicene Creed and of the controversy related to it.

inevitable, though in view of the complexity of the subject and all the theologians have had to say about it, my treatment has not really been long but rather short. Yet I would hope that it will serve as a safeguard, on the one hand against such an unthinking use of the doctrine as would tend towards tritheism, and on the other against a shallow impatience with the whole matter. I have tried to show you some of the concerns that were actually at stake, some of the convictions the Church was trying to express.

And if, at times, the whole may seem unreal to you, remember this: that the doctrine stands finally for the element of *mystery* in the Godhead. God 'dwells in unapproachable light'.[1] 'Great indeed, we confess, is the mystery of our religion.'[2] That is in itself an important truth about all our knowledge of God—that it is a very fragmentary thing, yielding but a tiny patch of light surrounded by ineffable mystery. The reason for the gladness we have as Christians is that through Christ and the Holy Spirit we know enough of the nature of God to enable us to trust even the utmost depths of its remaining mystery. That is what we confess with adoration and thanksgiving when after a psalm or canticle we sing or say the long-hallowed words: 'Glory be to the Father, and to the Son, and to the Holy Ghost; as it was in the beginning, is now, and ever shall be, world without end. Amen.'

[1] I Timothy, 6.16. [2] I Timothy, 3.16.